Drive • Navigate

MW01129272

Jack W. Peters

Editor

Joan Raymond
JoanRaymondWriting.com

jack@donorthmedia.com
www.donorthmedia.com
www.facebook.com/treasurequestjack/

PO Box 52, Walterville, Oregon 97489 USA

Second Edition, updated December 2020

ISBN 9798681523901 Amazon

DEDICATION

To the loving memory of

Fred Wayne Carnahan

1962 to 2008

An inspiration to anyone who knew him and whose hunting and fishing adventures were nothing short of legendary.

DISCLOSURE

Every effort has been made to ensure the accuracy of this information. The author and publisher assume no liability for loss caused by errors or omissions. Travel and navigation are potentially dangerous activities. The purpose of this manual is to teach off-road travel skills as well as to stress the importance of all users of this guide assuming the responsibility of understanding their own knowledge, abilities, and equipment.

SYMBOLS

Throughout this book, symbols indicate important tips or for what we consider the very least of what you should know. They include a light bulb for ideas, a nuclear symbol for caution, and a cross-bone skeleton for danger.

Other books in print by Jack W. Peters

The Goldfish That Barked,
Seven Actions to Distinguish Yourself for Success

Explosives and Blasting, 5th Edition

Explosives, IEDs and Breaching for Law Enforcement, 3rd Ed.

ACKNOWLEDGEMENTS

Special thanks to those who helped make this book possible.

Editor
Joan Raymond, JoanRaymondWriting.com

Initial Editor & Webmaster
Suzie Patterson, *Webmarketers.net*

Cover Photography

Nick Psomas, ApexSuspension.com (Ford Ranger front cover)
Photographer, Matthew Girgis

Marcos Soto-Montpellier, (Jack, NCE Land Cruiser rear cover)

Special Written Contributions

Gary and Monika Wescott, *Turtle Expedition.com*
Jens Stormer, Contributor, Photographer
Doug Shipman, *Ships Mechanical*

Photos and Consultation

Mark Badgerow
Christian Beck
Arne and Pam Beckman
Best in the Desert Racing Association
Bill Burke, *4-Wheeling America*
Ryan Burks, *Special Vehicles Group*, Oregon SAR Team
Amanda Carman, *Rogue Offroad*
Meg Chamberlain
Buzz Chandler, *Pacific Coast Rover Club*
Brett Cifaldi
Erik Claus, *Go2explr*
Jimmy Crawford
Ronny Dahl
Kaz Danielle
Chad and Brooke Dannon
Ricky David
Desert Turtle Racing
Nate Hunt, *BF Goodrich Racing*
Gordon Kallio, Photographer
Angela Gutherie

Eric Gwaltney
Tom Isaacs, Nuthouse Industries, LLC.
Steve Kiepert, AC7EC, Amateur Radio Specialist
Loyd 'Tom' Kruse, *Risky Business Desert Racing*
Seth & Kande Jacobsen, *Adventure Driven*
Lindi Jensen
Nicole Livering
Jack Mate, high-lift jack accessory
John Lucasey, *Gaasit.com*
Steve Lutz, *Rugged Routes.com*
Tony McLaren Desert Race Team
Kobus Mans, *Life Remotely.com*
John K. Miller, *Lane County SAR* Coordinator, Retired
Weston Miller
Aaron Paris, *Adventure Motors*
PCI Race Radios
Donald Perez
Pamela Petroff, *Pacific Coast Rover Club*
Joshua Provence
Darin Record
David Rod
Jeremiah Evans, *Expedition X Offroad*
Trail Nomads
Travis Rutherford, Photographer
Havas-Sarban, *Sand Ladders.net*
Steve Schoenfeilder, *Warn Industries, Inc.*
Rob Seubert Pro Truck 4724 Racing Team
Bob and Kelly Smith, Desert Race Team
Marcos Soto-Montpellier, *NCE Transportation*, Bolivia
SportsMobile, 4WD Van Conversions
Martha Tansy, *Off-Road Racing and Hunting*
Chris Tillaart
Adam Tolman
Discovery Channel's *Treasure Quest* TV Series
Scott Turnbull
Ujoint Offroad, Chris Steuber
Frank Watervoort
Benjamin Weight

CONTENTS

I. INTRODUCTION: DEATH ROAD

Accept the Challenge!

Let me take you on a little journey. You have prepared your truck to come along. You have spent years perfecting its parts and accessories. Bumper to bumper, lights, suspension, differential lockers and engine upgrades, the perfect off-road machine. Then it is time to outfit it with all the tools and supplies needed for the long trail. GPS, spare parts, high-lift jack, first aid, air supply with enough extra tools and gear to sag your leaf springs.

Now we are finally on the road, leaving the city traffic and lights behind for the great outdoors. Working our way through the countryside until we pull off on an inviting dirt road. Fresh air, until a perfect combination of dust, dirt and mud boil up from our tires as the double track dirt road twists and winds higher in elevation. We can now look down through high mountain passes to the spectacular views below.

Yungas 'Death Road,' Bolivia

Now the dirt road is becoming much rougher, with deeper tracks and puddles of water until we are dodging boulders and streams of water running through the road. As the road climbs, we decide to lock in the front axle for four-wheel drive.

The road drastically narrows to the point where the passengers' hearts race when they see straight down the cliff and tires skirt inches from the side of a partially collapsing roadbed. Our driving becomes a little slower and deliberate knowing that losing control could mean sliding off a mountain cliff.

Now, imagine that instead of driving your ideal off-road truck you now have a minivan that is only two-wheel drive. Instead of your nice seats with seatbelts, there are rows of benches filled with travelers with babies and children sitting on their laps. Your bead-lock wheels with neatly outfitted A/T tires have been traded for narrow stock steel wheels and bald mix-matched tires.

Headlights are approaching directly ahead, it's a semi-truck coming right at you. The off-road trail is actually a primary route for commercial and agricultural traffic. You are now on the *Death Road.*

Yungas Road, Bolivia

There is also an unknown element of road rules. Do you stay to the left, or right, who knows? You try to pull over on the narrow mountain pass but the truck in front of you persists to pressure you over to the muddy cliff wall where the truck passes you so close you fold in your rear-view mirrors as you hold your breath with only inches to spare before contact.

The next corner reveals a rancher herding a flock of sheep covering the road. You hammer the brakes as animals flee for the steep mountain banks to get out of the way as you negotiate your truck through the animals that holler out in protest.
Still driving on, you shake your head in disbelief wondering what you could possibly be running into next?

Around the next switchback are three large bulls standing in the roadway. They turn and offer a defiant look, saying they are not moving. Their horns are as wide as your side window and sharp enough to puncture your radiator. After honking and gradual nudging, the beasts finally move out the way allowing you to pass.

The sun has long dropped below the mountains and your latest LED light technology has been replaced by stock headlights squinting through cloudy scratched lenses. The road finally takes a decent, steeper and steeper, you shift down the transmission in the attempt to reduce as much speed as you can, giving the fading brakes as much needed relief as possible.

With a flash of lightning, the skies open up, smearing wipers into a flurry across a muddy windshield. You hear it before you see it. A crashing waterfall coming down the mountainside. Ahead, the road looks completely flooded. When you approach, headlights reveal a river flowing across the roadway.

Sacambaya River, Bolivia

It is unknown how deep the water is, and no one is the in the mood to walk across the rushing river in the cold night rain. Holding your breath once again, you venture the vehicle out into the water flowing before you. The van sinks lower and lower and you hear the engine labor through as the tires spin on the loose rocks and mud below.

Water is now over the tires and it is too late to turn around now.

At this point all you can do is pray the water is not entering the ignition system or even worse the air intake. Slowly, the vehicle rises out of the water as you see the bank head through the pouring rain. You let out a breath of relief when the front tires drive up the muddy bank.

Your eyes are heavy after driving though muddy roads until a slight glow of the sunrise moves up over the mountains. Up ahead is a group of vehicles with movement around them. You adjust your blurry eyes to see a roadblock ahead. Now what? Your mind races. Could it be the military, the locals assessing a road tax, or worse, banditos ready to relive you of all you have?

.   .   .

The example I laid before you appears dire. Certainly not the enjoyable afternoon outing you may have been expecting, but I brought you on this rather ominous journey to make some critical learning points.

First, this type of travel happens every day around the world. Drivers face difficult obstacles in often stock and poorly maintained vehicles, yet still successfully make it through.

Second, imagine how much more you can do with a properly equipped and maintained truck? Especially after some training and experience until your confidence soars to the point you feel you can take on the world's worst roads, or at least by starting with the ones in your own backyard?

I have been there. From managing a 4WD search and rescue in the woods of Oregon. To desert racing in Nevada and Baja Mexico. Navigating through the Himalayan jungles of India, to Death Road in Bolivia. It is true that most who own 4WD vehicles will never challenge themselves or their trucks, but sooner or later you will need these skills. Maybe a storm, you are stuck, someone gets lost, Murphy's Law sneaks upon you when you least expect it.

Accept the challenge. If I can learn to Drive, Navigate and Survive, you can too. Welcome to the journey that can be much more exciting than the destination.

Jack W. Peters

2. 4WD 101

High Tech or Low, Understand your Gears before Shifting

Travis Rutherford

A properly equipped 4WD truck will take to you places practically inaccessible by any other means of travel.

Four-wheel drive vehicles were invented and evolved out of necessity from the battlefields of WWII. After the war, *Jeep* vehicles were made available to the public who purchased them as fast as they could be made. Other manufactures like *Land Rover* soon followed and four-wheel drive trucks were sold around the world literally replacing the workhorse.

With an extra-drive axle, mud tires, and higher ground clearance, these trucks were perfect for hundreds of applications from hauling military hardware to taking the family camping. Surprisingly, over fifty years later, not much has changed. Technology has improved, and these vehicles have become much more comfortable if not luxurious. The basic mechanics and applications, however are much the same.

To fully appreciate these trucks and their capabilities, we'll first take a look at the mechanics to help understand what sets them apart from other vehicles. This will include the terminology and a look at the four-wheel drive systems available, including the various drivetrain components. We'll then review some of the more common four-wheel drive systems by manufacturer.

Four-Wheel Drive Systems

Unfortunately, four-wheel drive terminology is confusing. Phrases include *4x4, 4WD, all-wheel drive, permanent 4WD, part-time* and *full-time 4WD*, etc. These phrases are used by manufactures to describe drivetrain systems that power both front and rear wheels at the same time. But the confusion doesn't stop there due to the number of drivetrain systems with various levels of mechanical and electrical control.

Before buying or using a 4WD truck, it's important to understand the drivetrain that it offers. You will need to relay on this equipment to get you home, and the truth is, it is difficult to completely rely on a system without having a basic understanding of what's involved and how it works.

Four-wheel drive vehicles include extra drivetrain that allows power to both the front and rear axles through a transfer case. On a rear two-wheel drive vehicle, the engine powers the transmission, then a driveline powers the rear axle. On a four-wheel drive vehicle, the engine's power goes from the transmission to another gearbox known as the transfer case to direct power to drivelines that power both the front and rear axles at the same time.

 Four-wheel drive vehicles without locked differentials, only drive one wheel from the front and rear axle at the same time.

In two-wheel drive mode, the transfer case will power only one axle or power either the front or rear axle for all-wheel drive systems. Four-wheel drive is selected by shifting the transfer case into high or low four-wheel drive.

In four-high, power is transferred from the transmission through the transfer case to both front and rear axles at the same time. The gearing will most likely be the same as the gearing provided by the transmission.

Four-wheel drive high is best used when it is necessary to maintain some level of speed such as on loose gravel roads or in shallow snow.

For improved control, shifting into four-wheel drive low reduces the gear ratio considerably through the reduction gears in the transfer case. Shifting into four-wheel drive low, first gear, for the first time is an unforgettable feeling. The torque in your truck is unleashed as you creep along as it feels like you are driving a tractor. You might feel like you can drive through or climb nearly anything, and with a little practice, you just might.

First gear may feel better for stump pulling than starting out. Using second gear for taking off is usually best. Four-wheel low is best for sand, mud, climbing or any technical off-road driving. When in doubt, it is better to start off in four-wheel drive low for the simple reason that once you are committed to a challenging or technical bit of driving, you will most likely not have time to shift into four-wheel low.

Shifting into low range may cause you to lose valuable momentum, causing you to become stuck. This is because shifting the transfer case in most cases requires that the truck is stopped or at least moving very slowly. On traditional four-wheel drive trucks, it means getting out to switch over the front axle hubs.

Shifting into low range is not typically possible to do successfully in the middle of a hill climb or powering through a mud hole. It is often easier to drive in four-wheel low using a higher transmission gear, like third or fourth, but at least you always have the option to quickly shift down to a lower gear as needed.

 While four-wheel drive greatly improves traction in snow and ice, do not let it become a false sense of security because it does nothing to help with steering or braking.

Part-Time Four-Wheel Drive Systems

This is the standard four-wheel drive system for most older trucks and larger modern ones. In two-wheel drive, only the rear axle is powered. To shift into four-wheel drive, the driver needs to activate the front axle by locking the front wheel hubs.

Allowing the front hubs and axles to *freewheel* while in two-wheel drive reduces drag and helps improve mileage. The front hubs are locked manually (by turning the switch in the center of the hub of each front wheel), or electronically (by activating a switch on in the dash).
Once the front axle is locked, the driver can shift the transfer case into low or high range. The function of locking the hubs and shifting the transfer case is done while the vehicle is stationary.

Permanent All-Wheel Drive Systems

This system is common on many small to mid-sized SUVs. All-wheel drive is a higher tech, typically more complicated four-wheel drive system designed to improve traction for day-to-day driving. These vehicles can typically be switched from two to four-wheel drive, but when in two-wheel drive, the transfer case may alternate the power from to the front or rear wheels based upon road conditions.

A *central differential* transfer case is used to power both the front and rear axles at the same. The central differential works similar to an axle differential, as it allows the front and rear axle driveshafts to spin at different speeds while cornering on pavement. Some systems also use a mechanical or electronic means to transfer power to the axle most likely to provide the most traction.

One device for this is the *Viscous Coupling*. This is a silicone-based system that senses wheel slippage by the excess heat generated by the spin of a driveshaft to a slipping axle, then transfers power to the opposite axle's driveshaft.

Many light duty, economy, or smaller sport utility vehicles such as the *Subaru* line are all-wheel drive. If they do not have a low range transfer case option, so they are best suited for bad weather and *light* snow only.

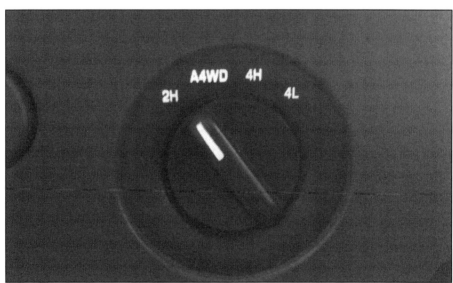

*4WD terms are confusing and can vary from different manufactures. For example, what is the difference between **A4WD** and **4H**? **A4WD** transfers power to the front or rear axle as needed but not both at the same time. **4H** and **4L** powers both axles at the same time.*

Computerized Four-Wheel Drive Options

Some modern four-wheel driving vehicles provide push button, computer-controlled options to match the current terrain conditions. This includes the *Land Rover Range Rover*, *Ford Raptor F150* pickups and other SUVs like the *Porsche Cayenne*. Push button options include Hill Decent (reduces tire skidding while traversing steep hills), Ice and Snow, Mud and Sand. My favorite is the *Raptor's Baja Mode* allowing for maximum traction on loose dirt roads for driving at speed.

These high-tech systems use the computerized ABS (Automatic Breaking System) that detects wheel spinning and slippage to instantly break the spinning wheel and redirect torque to the other wheels providing optimal traction and vehicle control.

Four-Wheel Drive Vehicle's Dirty Little Secret Number One

Four-wheel drive vehicles are only two-wheel drive. When the driver activates the transfer case, both front and rear axles drive the vehicle. The differentials have a ring and pinion gear assembly on each axle. These ring and pinion gear assemblies allow the axles to slip, allowing the outside wheel to spin faster while cornering. These slipping axle differentials only allow one wheel, per axle to power the truck at a time.

A vehicle traveling under normal conditions operates in one-wheel drive, shifting into four-wheel drive provides two-wheel drive as only one-wheel powers to the vehicle per axle. Again, this is because it is necessary for the outside wheels to turn faster when corning. To make matters worse, power is applied to the wheel that can spin the easiest. This means the differential transfers the drive power to the tire that has lost traction or contact with the ground.

On a technical trail, it is not uncommon to have both axles twisted, allowing both a front and rear wheel to spin freely allowing no power to be applied to the ground. There are two ways to deal with this problem. The first is a mechanical modification of adding locking differentials allowing both tires to be powered on each axle at the same time.

The tractor-like ability of true four-wheel drive provides awesome traction, but not without cost and risk of mechanical breakage. The second method is to learn to drive in a way where all tires are in contact with the ground for maximum control and traction. Check out the following chapter for more information on differential lockers.

Consumer based four-wheel drive trucks are still road-based vehicles and are not designed from the factory for serious off-road travel.

Four-Wheel Drive Vehicle's Dirty Little Secret Number Two

Stock four-wheel drive trucks and sport utility vehicles are not *really* off-road vehicles. They may have a little more ground clearance and suspension to give them a little more capability in mild conditions, but that's about it. There are a few exceptions to this as auto makers recognize people love to fix up and modify their trucks. It only makes sense to offer a model that has many of the upgrades already built in.

Some examples of this is the *Jeep Wrangler Rubicon* with locking differentials, the *Ford Raptor's* is *Fox* desert suspension and the *Chevy Colorado Z72* with lifted suspension, custom shocks, and a diesel engine option. Also, *Toyota* pickups and SUVs known around the world for outback reliability. Previous versions of capable trucks would have included the *Land Rover Defender* and the *Hummer H1*.

All great vehicles, but at a price. New can start from $45,000 to $85,000. And that is just the beginning, because even the most well-equipped trucks from the factory will still need upgrades and modifications. Stock motor vehicles do not make good off-road vehicles because they are made up of many complex mechanical, hydraulic, fluid, and electric systems built for general use.

From radiators to tires, these many somewhat-fragile vehicle systems are do not always hold up well to the abuse, stress and vibration from off-road driving. The weakest link theory applies to this application because if any one of the vehicle's systems is damaged, it will most likely disable the entire truck.

This is why a failed $.99 hose clamp can take out an exotic high-dollar race truck. This problem is combated in two ways. First is to prep a vehicle to make these systems as protected and durable as possible. The second is to drive in a way that allows you to get where you want to go while still preserving your transportation.

 Automatic or Manual Transmission? There are advantages to both. Auto is smoother off-road allowing constant power without a break in momentum from manual shifting. Manual shifting is more fun, gives more control, a little better gas mileage and can be push-started.

The Ultimate Off-Road Vehicle?

Is there an ultimate off-road truck? This has always been a subject of much discussion and debate. Most truck owners are fearlessly loyal to their favorite brand of vehicle. The truth is there are many factors to consider and each truck brand has its strong and weak points.

Maxum

Auto makers are building more capable trucks due to the buyer's strong demand for useful features. Chevy teamed up with AEV to offer real-world options on the new Colorado Bison. Beadlocks, snorkel, custom bumpers with built-in winch, at a 2.8 diesel, it is expedition ready from the dealer showroom floor.

Short, wheel-based Jeeps like the *Wrangler* have always been popular choices, but these small trucks are nearly impossible to take a family of four camping. Others might argue the mighty Hummer is the ultimate truck, but they are often too wide more many forest trails and can cost over $100,000.

Cost must be considered as a major issue. It is good to have the ability to buy a new truck, but if you do, your payment might be half of your mortgage and will you really enjoy yourself out on the trail in fear of the slightest scratch or dent? That can be nerve racking and take the fun out of off-road driving.

I always thought it was more fun to buy a good used truck, something with good bones and potential, then fix it up the way I want it.

Custom build a vehicle to what you are going to use it for and on a budget. And if you do get trail scratch or dent, it's not something you have to call the insurance company about. In fact, you wear it as a badge of honor from your rig surviving a great off-road adventure.

While working with the Indian Military the vehicle of choice was the Gypsy based off the Suzuki Samurai. Capable 4WD trucks don't need to be monsters. It is about the set up and learning to drive.

 Save money and heartache by selecting the right truck the first time. Be realistic about how much truck you need, where you are going to take it, and how much gear or persons you need to carry.

Before you go shopping, there are several points to consider:

- How and where are you going to drive it? Snow, desert, mud— different terrain types requires special modifications to assist with the challenging characteristics of each.

- How much room do you need? Are you taking a family or just your dog? How much gear do you need to take after considering the basic tools, recovery gear, survival gear and spare parts?

- How much money can you spend? The cost of the truck is just one aspect of the overall expense. The real money starts going out when making modifications, accessories, maintenance and repairs.

- How much mechanical work can you do yourself?

Vehicles that are driven off-road require about three times the maintenance of a passenger car. If you don't already, learn how to check and replace the truck's fluids, air filter, fuel filter and ignition parts. Preventative maintenance is less expensive than broken parts that can result from neglect.

Four-Wheel Drive System Components

Before you can consider purchasing and prepping a four-wheel drive truck, it's time to get down to basics with the definition of the primary drive terrain components:

Constant Velocity Joint (CV Joint)

Similar to compact drive shafts used to power independent axles. CV joints use a sealed large ball bearing housing to more smoothly transfer power to wheels moving at various angles. Typically used in Independent Front Suspension (IFS) four-wheel drive trucks.

Central Differential

Used in full-time 4WD systems to distribute power to both the front and rear axles in many mid-sized SUVs. The central differential allows using 4WD on pavement by requiring the front the rear axles to turn at different speeds. In two-wheel drive mode, power is directed to either the front or rear axle. Shifting into 4WD, splits the power to both the front and rear axles.

Differentials

The axle housing for the ring and pinion gears. The differential also contains the spider gears for an "open" differential or a "locker" for a locking differential. It is necessary to run an open differential under normal driving conditions. This is to allow the outside wheels to turn at a faster speed while cornering.

Driveshaft

The shafts transfer power from the transfer case to the front and rear axles. Driveshafts contain a u-joint on each end to allow the shaft to flex with the movement of the suspension. They also telescope for length adjustment as axles move up and down through their suspension travel.

Engine

Most truck manufactures offer a gasoline powerplant. Diesel motors have always been popular due to their simplicity, improved mileage and increased torque.

Diesel motors do not have electronic ignition systems and most older power plants are not computer controlled, making them more reliable in tough off-road conditions. Computer controlled motors can be chipped and tuned for more power or mileage. Unfortunately, diesel options have always been limited in the US market.

Full Time 4WD or All-Wheel Drive

A system that allows front or rear axles to power the vehicle as needed through a *Central Differential* or *Viscous Coupling* transfer case. Shifting into 4WD distributes the power to both the front and rear axles at the same time. These systems where designed for improved traction for day-to-day driving.

Independent Front Suspension (IFS)

A typical IFS four-wheel drive truck front suspension includes a differential with two independent axles connected to the differential and each front wheel by CV joints. This allows the front wheels to move up and down independent of each other. Typically considered smoother and not as durable as a solid axle system. Typically preferred by those who drive faster-moving vehicles such as desert pre-runners and racers.

Locking Differentials

Differentials are *open* unless they are *locked*. On an open differential, only one wheel drives the axle at a time which is the wheel that has the least resistance or traction. Locking differentials drive each wheel on the axle at the same time. Lockers are manual or automatic. Manual lockers are activated by air, electricity or a cable and the driver can turn on and off. Automatic or *Limited-Slip*, lockers are activated when extra torque is applied through a clutch system.

Locking Hubs

On a traditional four-wheel drive, the front wheels spin freely or *Freewheel* until the front hubs are locked. To place the vehicle into four-wheel drive, the front hubs need to be locked before shifting the transfer case into four-wheel drive. Locking hubs can be manual or electric. Manual locking hubs are identified as the round "Lock/Free" dial located in the center of the front hubs.

Part-Time 4WD

A traditional 4WD system in which the vehicle is powered by the rear axle only until the transfer case is engaged to distribute power to both the front and rear axle at the same time. Used for off-road or snow and ice only. Damage can result if this system is operated on dry pavement.

Solid Axle

Differential and axles are contained in one sold, ridged axle housing. Simple and rugged, but not as smooth as independent suspension because movement from one-wheel effects the opposite wheel. Typically preferred by more extreme wheelers who are willing to give up a little better handling for strength and simplicity.

Transfer Case

A gearbox used to engage both the front and rear drive axles. On a traditional four-wheel drive, a transfer case shifted into 2WD powers the rear axle only. Shifting into 4WD powers both the front and rear axle in high or low range. Rock crawlers use a *gear reducer*, a transfer case attachment to reduce the low range further.

Transmission

Gearbox behind the engine used for appropriate gear selection. The transmission shifts manually or is automatic. Each style has their pros and cons. Automatic transmissions tend to be smoother by not interrupting the momentum of power from manually shifting.
Also, the fluid torque convert absorbs shock to help reduce stress on the drivetrain. Automatic transmissions also free up shifting hand and clutch pedal foot.

Manual transmissions have their benefits too. More enjoyable to drive and control by manually selecting the gear you want to be in. No slipping torque convert also means a little better gas mileage. Manual transmission vehicles can also be push started.

U-Joint

"Universal joint" is a flexible coupling joint used at each end of drive shafts and CV joints.

Viscous Coupling

A fluid and clutch system used in a full-time, four-wheel drive transfer case. The system is activated from sensing friction from a spinning drive shaft to an axle that has lost traction. This activates a clutch system to distribute power to the opposite axle for better traction.

Unique Manufacture 4WD Systems

There are a multitude of vehicle manufactures, models and brands. Many of the 4WD/AWD trucks and SUVs fall into the "Cute-Ute" category. These vehicles do not have low range transfer cases and are best used for on-pavement, poor weather conditions.

The focus here is 4WD drive train systems that are most likely to be used for serious off-road or expedition travel. The following examples are some of the primary four-wheel drive systems that fall into this more capable four-wheel drive category:

Hummer H1

The primary powerplant is a GM 6.5L turbo diesel with an overdrive four-speed automatic transmission. It is all-wheel drive system with a 242 New Venture transfer case with locking high and low range.

Traction is provided mechanically and electronically through the *TorqTraq 4* (TT4) system where wheel spin in monitored and braking is applied to slipping wheels, applying traction to the opposite wheel on the axle. A differential includes a *Torsen II* limited slip system. A unique feature is the central tire inflation system (CTIS). This allows the tires to inflate or deflate while the truck is moving.

Chevy, Dodge, Ford, Toyota pickup

Most American-made full-sized pickups and SUVs use a traditional part-time, four-wheel drive system. Most transfer cases include gearing for 2WD high for pavement and 4WD high and 4WD low for off-road. Based on model and year, transfer cases can be shifted with a manual stick shift or electronically with a push of a button.

Ford Raptor Generation 1

These trucks included an *Off-Road Mode* button that is located just above the gear shift and can only be activated if driving less than five MPH. The rear differential is locked, engine response is increased, transmission up-shifts are delayed and less frequent to ensure that acceleration response is available for navigating obstacles.

The Off-Road Mode is complimented by Ford's *Advance Trac System*, that when in Off-Road Mode, the system is calibrated to enhance off-road driving performance.

The *Advance Trac System* button is located on the dash above the radio. The system includes ABS, RSC (roll stability control), and traction control. When is button is pressed and released, the truck is put into *Off-Road Sport* mode. All electronic nanny systems are still active, but traction control and roll stability control are less invasive and allow for more vehicle slip for more aggressive off-road driving.

For the driver's complete control of the truck, all traction assistance including traction control and roll stability control are shut off by pressing and holding the button.

Fun at your fingertips, the six driving modes of the Gen 2 Raptor. Personally, I think every truck should have a 'Baja' mode.

Ford Raptor Generation 2

This Raptor's drive mode system is much simpler and advanced with six different driving modes and three steering modes that the driver can toggle through. Driving modes include:

Normal (2WD) Ideal for everyday driving.

Sport (2WD) Higher shift points for higher engine revs, sport steering.

Weather (AWD) Auto 4WD, *Advance Trac* engaged for wet, snow, ice.

Mud-Sand (4WD H) Traction control off, rear differential lock engaged.

Baja (4WD H) Traction control off, open rear differential, quicker sifts.

Rock Crawl (4WD L) Rear differential lock engaged, front camera on.

Jeep Cherokee and Others

Jeep uses their own terminology to describe their own full and part time four-wheel drive systems:

Command-Trac Part-Time 4WD system with a high and low range. Transfer case is a NP 231.

Select-Trac Includes a high and low range, but the high range provides two options. 4WD part-time for off-road only, or 4WD full-time, capable of being used on the pavement. Transfer case is the NP/NVG 242.

Quad-Trac A full-time 4WD system using a Viscous coupling in a central differential with a high and low range. Transfer case was the Borg-Warner 1305/1339 from 1973 to 1979, then the NP 249 from 1948 to 1987.

Quadra-Drive Full-time 4WD system where a hydraulic pump clutched NVG 247 transfer case. The rear wheels are powered until spinning occurs, transferring power to the front axle. This system was combined with Jeep's *Vari-Lock* limited slip front and rear differentials.

Quadra-Drive II Full-time 4WD with a NVG 245 transfer case combined with electronic front and rear limited slip differentials.

Jeep JK Wranglers

When the new style four-door JK was release in 2007 it included a new ***Electronic Stability Program (ESP)*** system. It monitors the direction of the Jeep and can take corrective action if you find yourself sliding from oversteer or understeer. This is done by decreasing the throttle and applying brakes to more or more wheels to bring the vehicle back on track based upon where the steering wheel is pointing.

The ESP system is integrated with the steering wheel sensor, yaw sensor, lateral acceleration sensor and automatic brake actuator that can apply pressure to the four brakes independently. Other systems that are bundled with the ESP system include:

Electronic Roll Mitigation (ERM) An extension of the ESP programming that anticipates a potential roll over caused by oversteer but will not help much in an excessive side angle situation.

Traction Control System (TCS) Brakes are applied and throttle decreased to slow spinning tires during acceleration. There is a limited slip feature built into this programming that will apply some braking to one tire if it is slipping by redistributing torque to the tires that are not slipping. This limited slip feature is active even when the rest of TCS is turned off.

These systems are ideal for novice drivers in stock Jeeps. Increased tire size and lifts can affect their ability to work, and many modified Jeep owners turn these features off.

Auto manufactures have some form of traction control they brand under different names but basically work the same. Wheel sensors detect spinning wheels, apply braking to those wheels to transfer torque to the traction wheels.

Land Rover

The primary powerplant is the 3.9 to 4.5-liter aluminum V8. A four-cylinder diesel engine was an option, but rare in the United States. The *Defender* and *Discovery* use an open central differential transfer case for a full-time 4WD system with a locking high and low range. The *Range Rover* uses a Viscous Coupling transfer case for a full-time system.

The later model *Range Rover*, *Discovery II*, *Freelander* and *LR3* use an **Electronic Traction Control** (**ETC**) system. Wheel sensors detect slipping wheels then apply braking to provide traction to the opposite wheel.

The *LR3* and the 2003 and up *Range Rover,* includes *the Terrain Response* system where the driver essentially programs the vehicle to the terrain by selecting a driving condition switch. Settings include general, snow, mud, sand and rock crawl.

Based on driving conditions, this computerized system makes adjustments to engine, transmission, transfer case, anti-lock brakes and the rear differential. The system includes *Hill Descent Control* (HDC), that restricts vehicle speed during downhill runs.

Toyota FJ Cruiser, Land Cruiser, 4Runner

With a number of models available, Toyota SUVs come in full and part-time four-wheel drive systems.

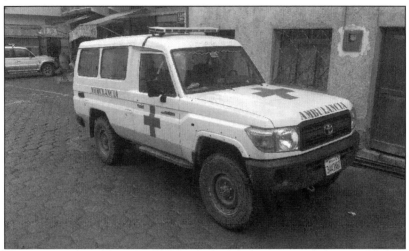

There are more Toyota SUVs and pickups around the world than any other brand. The remote town of Quime, Bolivia's medical center uses a Land Cruiser for an ambulance.

Since 2000, most Toyota SUVs are equipped with the **Active Traction Control (A-TRAC)** system. This electronic, button activated system provides traction by braking a spinning wheel, transferring power to the traction wheel. Since 2003, most SUV models include a *Torsen T-3* central locking differential. Improvements in this system provides 40% to 53% power to the front axle and 60% to 71% power to the rear axle based on slippage.

Will Your Next Pickup or SUV be Electric?

Do not laugh, the future is coming in faster than you might think. There are several electric auto makers that have highly capable pickups and SUVs in the works with claims of being available in possibly in 2021. These include the *Tesla Model P*, the *Rivian* SUV and pickup as well as the *Bollinger B1* SUV and *B2* pickup. *Ford* has taken notice to possibly by-pass its hybrid options and go to a straight electric F-150 pickup.

As someone who thinks the sound of a well-tuned engine is music, I am really trying to hate these things, but the numbers are impressive.

For example, according to *Rivian*, their *R1S* SUV and *R1T* pickup claim 0-60 in three seconds, 750 horsepower, 400-mile range, 7,700-pound towing capacity, advanced 4wd traction capabilities and able to ford one meter of water!

These electric trucks are not cheap, but there are federal and state tax rebates that will help and think of the money you are not spending in fuel. You do have to charge them taking 10 hours on slow or 70 minutes on rapid. You do have to pay by the kilowatt hours to charge and even homebased solar charging stations save money, but still not free with considerable upfront costs to set up. The cost kilowatts hours (KWh) are approximately 11¢ to 17¢ each. Instead of MPG it's the cost of Kilowatt hours per 100 miles. Range is going to be affected by driving style and accessories that burn electricity like air conditioning and headlights. In really rough numbers, it is still going to cost you about $10 to travel 200 miles.

Rivian R1S SUV and R1T Pickup   *Bollinger B2 SUV looks inspired by the Land Rover Defender.*

Tesla's P model high tech looks maybe inspired by Space X.   *Even the F-150 is going electric.*

For off roaders, these electric vehicles are a little hard to wrap your head around. No intake, no exhaust, no radiators, no engine oil and many other maintenance parts are gone. Instead computer circuits, batteries and electric motors that cannot be repaired in the field, especially off-the-grid.

There are more charging stations in remote areas that will help with some 'running out of electricity anxiety,' but that still may not help you where you want to drive. It will be very interesting to see how these vehicles will be accepted and how they will do when put to the test.

The Least You Need to Know

- Four-wheel drive terminology and technology can be confusing. Understand what system you need to use your truck to its fullest capacity in the field.

- Four-wheel drive systems are part-time or full-time. Understand the pros and cons of each to determine what might be the best for your application.

- Four-wheel drive trucks only drive two wheels at a time (one on each axle), unless there are locking differentials.

- Even the best-built four-wheel drive trucks are still somewhat fragile and can easily break down from the beating of off-road driving.

- Before purchasing or driving an off-road truck, take the time to understand the drivetrain system, parts and components to help determine the best options for your application.

- Consider that your near future off-road vehicle could be electric. Yes, they are expensive, but you can make a lot of payments with the money you are not spending on gas or diesel.

3. VEHICLE MODIFICATION AND PREPARATION

Off-Road Trucks are Built More Than Bought

First things first, before you start prepping a vehicle, make sure you have a good base to work from. A truck that is structurally sound that has the capability to do what you want it to. It's also an issue of cost vs. price. Ultimately it is less expensive to purchase a truck in good mechanical condition with many of the modifications you would like already done than the constant downtime and expense of multiple upgrades and repairs.

There is nothing like building a truck however, just the way you want and need it for off-road use. Regardless of the vehicle you buy or build, be sure it is well maintained and in good overall mechanical condition. First, we will look at areas to continually inspect, before and after off-road excursions. Then we will be a look at a variety of practical modifications and upgrades that will help you get there and back home.

Inspection Areas

Spend some time under the hood and under your truck to learn where the various components are and for any signs of leaking or damage. Check out what is protected by skid plates and what looks vulnerable to damage. Check the fluid levels for engine oil, transmission fluid, radiator fluid, battery water level and window washer fluid. Also be sure your lights, brakes, heater/defroster and wipers all work.

 Do a walkaround and look everything over carefully before and after every off-road run. Pop the hood and crawl underneath to check fluid levels, and for damage and leaks.

Areas to pay special attention to include:

Differential Housings

This is where the ring and pinion gears are in the center of solid axles. These housings are typically the drivetrain component with the lowest ground clearance. Trucks with front and rear solid axles are often offset from each other.

For example, the rear differential is in the center and the front is located off to the left or right side. Many *Land Rover* trucks have both front and rear differentials offset to the passenger side.
Know where the differentials are to know how to best approach driving over obstacles.

Exhaust System
Be sure the mufflers and pipes are mounted securely without hanging too low to catch on rocks and obstacles.

Fuel Tank
Fuel tanks are often mounted to protrude below the trucks frame at the rear of the vehicle. Unfortunately, this position leaves the tank a target for impact while crossing obstacles and during descents.

Oil Pans
A four-wheel drive vehicle will have three lower hanging oil pans. One each for the engine, transmission and the transfer case. If these do not include factory skid protection, consider purchasing aftermarket skid plates.

Radiator and Hoses
Keep an eye out for damage and leaks through the cooling system. Old hoses and belts can easily be replaced and when doing so, replace the cheap factory spring loaded hose clamps with aftermarket ones you can tighten down. Still-functioning belts and hoses should be saved for emergency repairs.

Steering Assembly
One of the most fragile parts to become damaged is the tie-rod. This is the linkage from the steering box to the spindles at the front wheels. This linkage is front and center, typically poorly protected and easily damaged.

Maintenance

Now that you have a better understanding of your truck's components, be sure they are properly maintained and in good operating condition. It pays to learn how to do much of the maintenance work yourself. This knowledge will be crucial on the trail where it is often necessary to make repairs. Even if you are not mechanically inclined, with a little practice, most of the basic work can be done by the newest of mechanics. Tasks ranging from changing the oil, belts, spark plugs and fuel filter can be quickly done in the driveway with simple tools.

If you are unable to do your own maintenance, find someone competent who can. Ask questions to learn more about your vehicle on an ongoing basis.

It is a good idea to replace maintenance parts before they go bad. These parts include fan belts, hoses, fuel filters, etc. Keeping these parts provides spares to keep on board.

 Doing your own basic maintenance will go a long way in recognizing problems and making repairs on the trail.

The following systems and components requiring ongoing inspection and maintenance:

Air Filter

Inspect filter, clean and replace as necessary. Factory style paper filters should be changed every year for optimal performance and gas mileage.

Battery

Off-road driving can shake the guts out of a standard battery. Consider a closed cell vibration-resistant brand. Check the water level in open cell batteries. Be sure the connectors are tight and clean.

Exhaust System

Check for crushed tubes, broken welds, and hangers.

Fuel Filter

This is a part that should be changed no less than every two years and is much easier to do in your driveway than out of the trail. Clogged fuel filters will stop you dead in your tracks. Before choking off completely, a restricted filter will stress your fuel pump. Check this item if your truck's engine will turn over but not start.

Oil and Filter

Scheduled oil changes are fine for asphalt, but for off-road, change it after every hard, dusty run.

Universal 'U-Joints'

U-joints connect each end of your driveshafts and allow them to flex with the suspension travel. When they start to go out, an ever-increasing vibration can be felt through the truck. When they go out, they often break apart potentially causing considerable damage as a loose end of a driveshaft whips around unrestrained, damaging everything in reach.

U-Joints can break apart because there are not properly lubricated. They contain grease Zerk fittings that are often missed by mechanics and quick lube centers. No shame in reminding them to grease the drive shafts up good. If you do not know if your u-joints have ever been replaced, do it now as a matter of preventative maintenance. You might be surprised on how much smoother your truck drives.

Tires

Inspect for leaks, gouges and punctures. Also be sure your tires are up to the proper inflation on the blacktop for increased safety and fuel mileage.

Tune Up Parts

Distributor cap, rotor, plugs, wires and fan belts. Change these parts before they go bad, then save the used parts for emergency spares. Use silicone glue to seal the distributor cap, spark plug wires and wiring connectors.

 Replace maintenance parts (like belts, hoses, distributor cap) before they completely wear out so they can be saved as emergency spares.

 Modifying an off-road truck is rarely ever complete. It's a never-ending investment of time and money and just when you think you're finished, you start all over again.

Modifications

True off-road vehicles are not bought, they are built. In fact, modifying a truck seems to be a never-ending cycle of aftermarket parts and improvement. Once one aspect of the truck is done, it is time to move to the next. One part or modification triggers the next until you come full circle and you start the process over again.

That is the dirty and often expensive reality of it if your rig is used off-road. Is it necessary to reach your credit card limit with the latest extreme modifications? No, probably not. It all depends where you want to go, how you drive and what level of durability and reliability are needed.

With the great variety of options for aftermarket truck parts and accessories, choose upgrades wisely that will provide the best improvements necessary for off-road survivability. Off-road vehicles follow the weakest link theory.

Meaning the weakest link in the truck will most likely break first. Think about modifications and improvements as continually trying to upgrade your rig's most venerable part.

Many of the parts and modifications are based on more appearance than function. The modifications being referred to here are based on practical improvements to complement backcountry driving. There is a saying, "Chrome doesn't get you home." This is true, but nothing wrong with having a good-looking truck. Before spending money on *bling*, check out making these basic improvements:

Air Compressor
On-board air is useful for activating ARB differential lockers and refilling tires. Air can also be used for power tools if your reserve tank is large enough. Most compressors are 12-volt. Some use belt-driven air conditioning compressor pumps, although they will provide an additional drag on the engine that may slightly reduce performance and mileage.

Air Filter
Going to an aftermarket air filter is often the first modification that is done. This is because a gaussian-based (*K&N* style) filter will improve airflow with gains in performance and mileage. Add a snorkel system to make it even better by keeping water out and colder outside air in your airbox for better performance. Consider a pre-filter for extra dusty or sandy conditions. This would include an oiled foam or nylon wrap to cover the primary filter.

Bumpers
A heavy-duty front bumper is an ideal platform for a winch, lights and pull points. An aftermarket rear bumper is an ideal platform for carrying the spare tire, high-lift jack, backing lights and antennas.

Exhaust
Headers improve mileage and performance and can be emission modification legal. Older clogged and restricted catalytic converters can be replaced with free-flow aftermarket ones. Larger exhaust tubing and free-flowing mufflers also improve mileage and performance.

Run tubing up and out of the way to exit in a safe location. Some serious off-roaders are running the exhaust out through a rear quarter-panel, preferably through the protection of a wrap-around rear bumper.

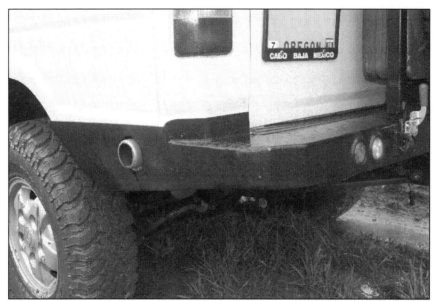

Tail pipe ran through the rear bumper to keep it up and out of the way.

Fuel Cans

Carrying extra fuel is a practical accessory, especially when driving loaded-down trucks getting just over double-digit fuel mileage. The best set up is on swing-out rear bumper gates that allow you to carry a spare tire and a jerry can or two up and out the way.

Good to get fuel can holders that lock down, this one is from Smittybilt.

Military surplus cans work great like the NATO 20-liter cans. I also use the U.S. 5-gallon water can that will fit in the same rack. There are several fuel can mounts on the market. Get one that locks, with the price of fuel, and cans, it may not be long until they are gone.

RotopaX

RotopaX makes fuel, water containers in multiple sizes that can be mounted on roll bars and racks. They also make matching sized containers for first aid and storage.

There has not been much innovation in fuel can technology in 50 years until now. *RotopaX* has developed a modular fuel container system that is slender and stackable, in different sizes, even color coded. Two containers at a time can be secured with twist lock down system that allows cans to be mounted on any vehicle about anywhere.

GPS Receiver
Powered by the truck's 12-volt system with a remote antenna if necessary, a dedicated GPS receiver frees up your phone to make navigation safer and much more effective.

Jack - Floor
Off-road racers, pre-runners and chasers tend to like floor jacks. These are possibly faster to deploy and less cumbersome to use. Like high-lifts, they are heavy and require mounting brackets to lock down.

Pro Eagle

Floor jacks are preferred for the desert race and chase crowd.

Jack - High-lift
These are heavy, clumsy, yet very necessary. Great for changing tires in soft terrain as well as a hand-winch for getting unstuck. Our 4WD search & rescue team also trained with them to be used as a 'Jaws of Life' for opening turned over cars.

4 Wheel Parts

High-lift jacks are the off-road standby. 6,000 pounds of lifting power with enough height to get stuck trucks out of sand and mud.

Rogue OffRoad, Amanda Carman

For the off-roader who has everything, consider this ARB hydraulic jack. A smoother, safer and more expensive alternative to the traditional high-lift jack.

Lights

A practical improvement for anyone who may need to drive off-road at night. Understand that lights come in three varieties: Halogen, HID and LED. Also understand how to wire them up correctly in the following Chapter 4.

Lift Kit

A three to four-inch lift is typically enough to fit larger tires and provide the additional suspension travel necessary for off-road driving. Higher lifts can throw off the driveline and suspension geometry as well as making the truck too top heavy.

Viber Motorsports

The advantage of popular Jeeps and trucks is there are so many aftermarket lift kit options available. Viber professionally installed this Teraflex 3" lift with arms and Fox Reservoir shocks.

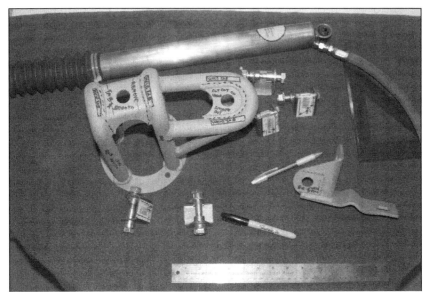

Owners of popular Jeeps and pickups have it easy when it comes to aftermarket lift kit options. For the Land Rover, it was lots of fabrication to create a prerunner dual reservoir shock system.

Shy away from spacers and blocks. Look for a high-quality complete kit, that includes shocks, brackets, and hardware to do it right.
While lift kits are one of the most popular modifications, they are not stand alone. Lifting a truck sets off a domino effect of other needed modifications that include longer stainless-steel brake lines, bushings, and a front-end alignment.

When it is time to get serious, shock reservoirs are used to give the shocks an expanded oil capacity. This helps keep the oil cooler, and shocks from fading after miles of whoops and bumps.

Lockers

One of the primary improvements to greatly increase your truck's off-road ability. Locker systems also replace the typically weak spider gear assembly.

Manual lockers are activated by air, cable or electricity. They require extra mechanics and electronics, but their positive "on/off" function is considered best for serious off-roading. Air lockers like the *ARB* utilize an air pump to activate the locker that can also be used for filling deflated tires.

ARB air lockers are ideal because they lock the differential with the push of a button although they do require an air compressor.

Automatic or *limited-slip* lockers use a clutch system that may lock the axle while the vehicle is traveling in a straight line or when additional torque is applied. If you need the highest level of traction, get both front and rear differential lockers. With several locker options available, select the best style to best match your driving conditions.

Pull Points

Pull points need to be strong enough to attach a tow strap and be jerked out of the mud by a multi-ton truck using all the power they have. In the front, it is good to use two so the load can be balanced. Pulling from only one, greatly increases the chance of damaging the bumper or frame.

In the rear, a pull point attachment that fits in a 2" towing receiver is ideal. It is attached to the frame and designed to take the most amount of load without damaging the vehicle. Never use a tow ball.

Quadratec

Front pull points should be in paired to better distribute the load.
In the back, a pull point for the 2" receiver is ideal.

Rack – Bed

Bed racks make an ideal mounting platform to organize the expedition gear you want to take with you. Roof top tents are mounted to the top. The side bars are used to mount cargo boxes, jacks, fuel/water containers, shovels, and sand ladders.

Bed racks make sense because after mounting all that equipment securely, you still have a pickup bed left for more storage. Bed racks come in two heights, cab height and ¾. Cab height provides more room in the bed but places the RTT in the airstream further disrupting aerodynamics. The ¾ height keeps the tent on a lower profile.

Tom Isaacs

This Jeep Gladiator is nicely equipped with RTT, fuel containers, and storage boxes mounted on a Nuthouse Industries bed rack.

Rack – Chase

Desert pre-runners and chasers use open bed racks making tires, tools, fuel cans and jacks open and quickly accessible. Every tire, box and container is secured with heavy ratchet straps to keep everything locked down for hundreds of off-road miles at speed.

Outlaw Off-Road

Rack – Roof

Roof racks or over-the-spare-tire racks are ideal for creating space for expedition essentials from tents, fuel cans, coolers and camping cargo. Roof racks also make a great platform for popular roof top tents and awnings. As practical as these racks are, they do come at a price.

Even an empty roof rack will destroy any aero dynamics you may have had anyway, dropping the gas mileage by at least 1 MPG and overloading a roof rack can be dangerous. Adding a couple hundred or more pounds to a roof rack will make your truck top-heavy requiring extra caution when off road driving. Practically speaking, however, with smaller vehicles with people and gear, you need the extra storage space.

Roof racks are great for storing expedition gear but make your truck drive top heavy which can be dangerous for off-roading.

Cargo bay shelves and drawers are a good option to stack more gear in the rear of the truck. It keeps gear safe and dry while lowering the center of gravity.

Radio

Do not count on your cell phone and CBs or Family Service Radios (FSRs). They don't have the range to work much beyond convoy travel. Serious backcountry or desert race support communication requires a VHF commercial band or HAM radio.

Rock Sliders

Practical body armor, these metal rails mount under door stills for lower side protection.

Skid Plates

Metal plates used to protect the most vulnerable of engine and suspension components. This includes oil pans, steering linkage and differentials.

LOD Rock Sliders

Rock sliders protect lower stills and doors from expensive body damage. Skid plates protect the other vitals underneath.

Snorkel

Designed to help keep water out of the air intake, drawing air out of the engine bay provides a couple of other benefits. The engine runs more efficiently on cold air due to a higher oxygen content. Drawing the air higher also provides cleaner air with less opportunity of water splashing in.

NCE Transportation, Bolivia

No downside to running a snorkel. Colder, cleaner air being scooped in providing high pressure oxygen directly into the airbox.

47

A forward scoop system provides positive air pressure to help the engine, but will also take in rainwater so it is critical the air filter box has a way to drain the water out fast enough that it will never flood the filter element. Do not let a snorkel give you a false sense of security. You should never drive in water deep enough that would flood your air box and electronics anyway.

Tires

Serious off-road tires come in patterns of All Terrain or Mud Terrain or some combination in between. The All-Terrain is for general off-road conditions while the Mud-Terrain has a more aggressive open lug design. The two primary theories in tire selection are a narrow tire to cut through loose terrain to more solid ground or wide tires that float on top of mud, sand and snow. Narrow tires might work fine if only driving through less than a few inches of snow or mud.

The practical problem to that is it does not take long to get into much deeper muck with no solid ground in reach to dig down to. The limited footprint narrow tires provide also makes them perform poorly in sand and dirt.
In contrast, a wider tire footprint helps stability with more rubber to the ground contact. They also provide a greater level of floatation to stay on top of loose terrain instead of getting stuck into it. This is exactly why airing down tires dramatically improves off-road traction.

Most off-road tires come in some variation of
All-Terrain on left and Mud-Terrain on right.

Improvements in tire tread design have allowed more aggressive tires to provide a quieter and better handling ride. Running tubes inside tires can also help maintain low air pressure if aired down below 12 pounds.

As far as tire size, everyone generally wants to run the largest they can fit. Larger tires provide greater ground clearance and help suck up off-road terrain through the ability to roll over larger obstacles. The downside is that larger tires also suck up horsepower and gas mileage. Ring and pinion gearing should also be lowered to maintain close to the stock gear ratios once tire size is increased three or more inches. Also, make sure the larger tires will not rub in your wheel wells.

Wheels

Cast alloy and aluminum wheels save on weight but bend easily, especial if tires are aired down. If bent, cast wheels can crack while spun aluminum wheels can sometimes be beaten back to shape. Bent wheels provide a harsh ride. Beadlocks provide a way to secure the tire to the wheel as well as give the wheel more strength.

When purchasing wheels, the best size for off-road is in the 16-17" range. This gives you a taller tire for better traction. Also consider the offset. This is the measurement of the distance from the hub mount surface to the centerline of the wheel.
Zero offset is the hub mount surface even with the wheel's centerline. Positive offset is when the hub mount surface is toward the face of the wheel.

Beadlock wheels look great and bolt the tire to the wheel. This helps the tire from rolling off the bead when aired down.

Negative offset is when the hub mount surface is toward the backside of the wheel's centerline. A negative offset is typically preferred for off-road vehicles as a wider stance increases stability.

Beadlock wheels are used to clamp the tire to the wheel. This helps prevent the aired-down tire from rolling off the bead while corning. External beadlocks use the distinct bolt-lined ring.

 Stick with 16-17" wheels for off-road. These provide a taller tire that can be aired down for traction. 20" and larger wheels are for the street, as their tires are too short to be practical off-road.

Winch

Purchase a winch with a minimum pound rating appropriate for your truck's weight. Installing a winch means a new front bumper and an updated electrical charging system.

 The electrical system is one of the off-road vehicle's most complex networks, often needing modifications and all prone to failure. Consider what electronic accessories will be used before updating batteries, alternators, and wiring.

10,000 lb Husky winch with updated synthetic line on the Rover.

For more information and products visit our friends at 4 Wheel Parts, www.4wheelparts.com/

The Least You Need to Know

- Constantly inspect vital truck parts, systems and components, before and after off-road driving.

- Preventative maintenance saves money and breakdowns on the trail.

- Learning how to maintain your truck is easier than you might think and is important to help keep your truck running on the trail.

- Replacing critical parts before they go bad and saving them provides emergency spare parts.

- Off-road rigs are built on an ongoing basis. Do your homework to plan the modifications needed for your application.

- Plan on spending more time and money than imagined to ensure the aftermarket parts are installed and dialed in properly.

4. LIGHTING AND ELECTRICAL MODIFICATIONS

Electronics are the Second Half of Truck Building.

After the lift kits, bumpers and all the hardware are planned, it is time to get serious about the electrical system and the many accessories expected to operate from it. From lights, winch, GPS, radios, and refrigerators to so many other power-using add-ons. To make them work reliably and safely, they must be installed correctly using the correct electrical components. This includes using the proper gauge wire, fuses, and relays to keep accessories working when you need them most.

Accessories Planning

With so many accessories available, we suggest pre-planning on which ones will be installed, either now or possibly in the future. Then building an electrical system around the power output and storage needed. This will include the following:

1. Battery or batteries
2. Upgrading to a high-output alternator
3. Adding an axillary fuse box
4. Adding relays
5. Running heavy wire cables through out
6. Adding a labeled switch panel

The following list includes possible electronic upgrades to consider. Have a look and make your own list. Once you have an electrical accessory plan, you can design the components to work right the first time. Doing so will save considerable time and money as well as help ensure your electronics work when you need them the most.

12-volt lighter plugs	110 power inverter	Air compressor
Amateur radio	Axillary lights	Back-up lights
CB radio	Driving lights	Fog lights
GPS receiver	Gauges	Laptop-tablet
Refrigerator	Satellite radio	Stereo & amps
Trailer wiring	Winch	Work lights

Electrical Components

Alternator

The alternator generates electricity for the system and its output is rated in amps.

Multiple accessories require high-output alternators with high battery capacity to store the energy being generated. Factory alternators for trucks and SUVs are typically at least 100-amps.

Companies like Promaster make high-output alternators for nearly any application designed to use factory mounting points and wiring harness for easy instillation.

For example, a 100-amp alternator with a single battery can run a winch for five minutes, but the alternator could require nearly a half an hour of engine running time to completely restore its voltage.
The problem is if the battery voltage drops below 9.5, the engine may not start.

When operating high electricity use accessories like winches and lights, you would want to keep the engine running anyway, but a higher capacity alternator will help keep the battery charged much faster. High-output alternators are typically 135 to 200 amps.

Fortunately, there are a number of factory and aftermarket options for higher capacity alternators that are bolt on and plug in. For example, the Ford F150 has a 157-amp alternator with a factory option of 200 amps. When it is time to replace or upgrade, shop around and find the best power plant with the output you need.

Battery Choice
Not much worse than being stranded with a dead battery. If your battery is getting close to four years old or showing signs of weakness, change it!

If you are not sure, put a multimeter or voltmeter on the battery terminals, it should read close to 13.6 volts. If your battery is newer and still not holding a charge, check the alternator. Be sure battery hardware is in good order. More misstarts are caused by loose and corroded battery terminals than anything else. Clean the battery terminal posts thoroughly and coat them with *WD-40*.

It is better to purchase a battery on your terms when wait until it's an emergency and you get stuck with whatever is available at the local auto parts store. Closed cell AGM batteries are best for off-road use. No need to fill them with water so they do not leak. They are also more vibration resistant and can be mounted in the cab.

Ensure that batterie(s) are bolted down tight with no ability to work loose and short out. Install a voltmeter to keep track of the health of your charging system. If everything is working properly, the voltage reading should be approximately 13.6-votls. A digital gauge is best by providing voltage within a tenth of a volt to more easily measure subtle changes in charging or discharging.

These batteries are called **AGM (Absorbed Glass Mat)**. Example brands include *Optima, Odyssey* and *Exide Edge.* AGM batteries are more expensive, but their increased power, life span and vibration resistance make them worth the investment for off-road use.

While more battery manufactures are entering the AGM market, the two primary brands are Optima and Odyssey.

Regardless of the brand or style of battery, understand how they are measured so you can compare and make the best purchasing decision.

Size   Batteries are sized by an international group number. For example, group 24 or 36, etc. Regardless of your vehicles recommended group size, get out the tape measure and determine the maximum size of battery you can fit under the hood.

If the hold-down hardware is weak or corroded, now is the time to replace that too with hardware strong enough to make sure the battery will not move. For extreme use, consider an aftermarket battery tray from a company such as *RuffStuff*.

When comparing batteries there are three primary indicators you should know:

CCA (Cold Cranking Amps) This is the primary measurement used and is defined as the number of amps a battery can crank at 0° F can deliver for 30 seconds while maintaining a minimum voltage of 7.2-volts.

CA (Cranking Amps) The number of amps a battery at 32° F can deliver for 30 seconds while maintaining a minimum voltage of 7.2-volts.

RCM (Reserve Capacity Minutes) The minutes a battery at 80° F can deliver a continuous 25-amp current while maintaining 10.5-volts.

Life Remotely.com

Dual batteries are best for running multiple accessories. Aftermarket battery trays help fit two under Jeep and midsize truck hoods.

Running Dual Batteries

If you have room, dual batteries are ideal to double your amperage storage capacity. One battery is dedicated to the engine and factory electrical functions while a second deep-cycle battery is used for powering all the energy consuming accessories like lights, winch and refrigerator. Even if you wear the auxiliary battery down, your primary battery can still start the engine. Aftermarket battery tray manufactures like *RuffStuff* allow dual batteries in tight engine bays.

For dual batteries, an isolator is used to transfer the alternator's output to the lowest charged battery. The other advantage is that it 'isolates' one battery from the other so one cannot discharge the other.

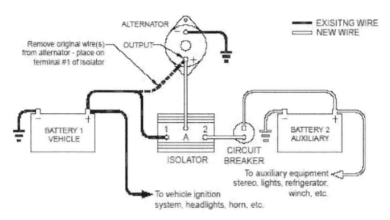

Battery isolators keep one battery from discharging the other. With this system, the auxiliary battery is dedicated to accessories so the primary battery will have enough charge to start the engine.

Auxiliary Fuse Box & Wiring

A rough and dusty off-road environment is the ultimate test to electronics. Bolting on lights and other accessories is the fun part. Now the real work begins as you select fuses, relays and wiring everything up carefully.

This is critical because they must work when needed most. The installation must be clean, allowing electronic gear to be plug-and-play, yet easily removed. Every last connection needs to be securely crimped or soldered, then wires need to be neatly wrapped or covered before being secured with zip ties and wire loom clamps.

Fuse box

Determining how many accessories used is important to determine the size of the fuse box needed. Finding a location to mount an auxiliary fuse box can be challenging. It's best to mount them inside the cab or at least out of the way of water and mud to provide them as much protection from the elements as possible.

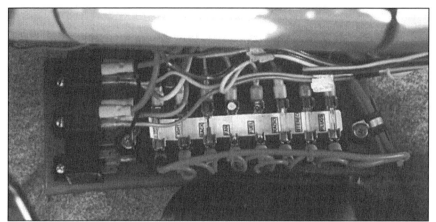

This is an auxiliary fuse and relay panel for a prerunner Bronco. The glass fuses are old school, but easier to find and replace blown fuses.

Another example of an auxiliary fuse and relay system in a Land Rover. The idea is keeping it organized, labeled and clean.

The distance from the battery that powers the fuse box will determine how heavy of a wire gauge is needed. When running multiple auxiliary circuits, it's always better to go too heavy than too light. A smaller gauged battery cable may be best if there is any distance between the battery and fuse box.

If possible, have the fuse panel next to the relays so they can all be wired together in the same area. It is also good to label the fuses and relays for each accessory or light system so any troubleshooting can be done as easy as possible.

There are several aftermarket prewired switch and fuse panel systems that make this job so much easier and cleaner.

Just pick out the rocker switches with the correct illuminated label, install the correct amp fuse, and just plug the wires into the lights or accessories.

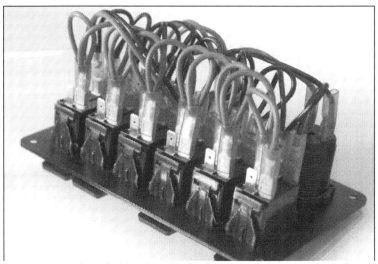

We recommend prefabbed switch plates to let someone else to do much of the tedious work for you. Labeled illuminated switches can be purchased for any accessory you can think of.

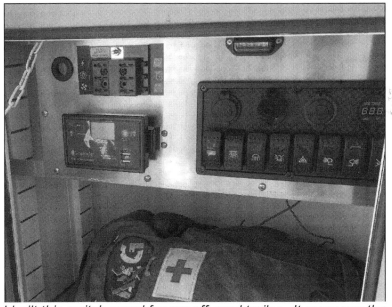

I built this switch panel for my off-road trailer. It manages the 12-volt battery and solar system with switches for work lights and the water pump for the kitchen sink.

For the ultimate high-tech cool switch setup, Switch-Pro has an 8-switch, backlight flat panel that that can be mounted almost anywhere and is plugged into a remote-control box.

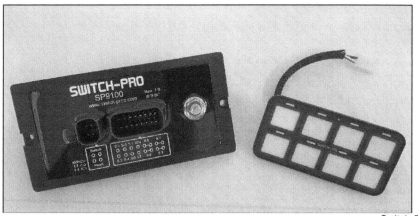

Switch-Pro

Running Wire

The number one rule of off-road wiring is no spaghetti! An inspection of your engine compartment and under-dash should reveal nothing but neatly bundled wires wrapped in wire looms and secured with lots of cable zip ties. Wire should end with securely crimped or soldered connections protected by shrink-wrap.

Clean wiring is important for several reasons. Looking better goes without saying, but it is also easier to trace and less likely to have a bad connection or short out. Worst case scenario, bad wiring can cause serious electrical damage or even catch your truck on fire. If you are not comfortable doing the wiring, have it done by a professional company like one that wires accessories for police and emergency vehicles.

We all wish our wiring could be as clean as the
'Desert Guy' did on his Baja Bug.

A great way to keep wiring clean is to run cables of wire instead of individual wires. For example, wiring a GPS NMEA data transfer requires four wires: positive, negative, data in and data out. If you are mounting an amateur radio in the same location, you need two more wires that are positive and ground.

Computer and home supply stores sell cables with multiple wire combinations of two and up. Cables of wires can be purchased in bundles of 4 to 8 wires per wrap. Extension cords have three heaving wires and provide an inexpensive and durable way to run power under the frame to the rear of the vehicle and other external applications.

If running wires under the truck or through an exposed engine bay, consider using extension cord cables. Cables work great because they can include heavy gauge wires and a thick rubber or plastic shield. For example, when wiring a 12-volt lighter plug in a rear cargo bay, I used a three 12-gauge wire cord. Two of the wires I soldered together at each end making one larger wire. The third wire was used to power a relay for backing lights.

Here is a chart to help determine the proper gauge of wiring for different amp loads:

10 Amp:	18/16 Gauge
15 Amp:	14 Gauge
20 Amp:	12 Gauge
30 Amp:	10 Gauge
40 Amp:	08 Gauge
60 Amp:	06 Gauge

Running wires and coax to a roof rack can be tricky. I have four coax cables and a cable with three heavy wires for lights. I did not want to drill a one-inch hole in the roof, so I decided to run the wires in a bundle externally up the front windshield pillar. All the wires run up through the engine compartment and are wrapped with a black plastic spiral wrap loom cover. The loom is zip-tied to the one-inch square *3M* adhesive tabs that have a slot for a cable zip tie to go through.

A grinding stone drill bit was used to wobble out an existing plastic and metal hole allowing the bundled wires to go into the engine bay. Where the wires go through the holes, they are protected by one-inch rubber grommets and then silicon glued to seal them up and prevent them from fraying.

An easy way to check your wiring is to use a voltmeter and test your voltage on the alternator terminals at 2000 RPMs. Then check the voltage on the positive wire behind the load, (ideally keeping the ground lead in the same place).

If the voltage difference is greater than one volt, you may need to upgrade your light wiring as well as check and clean wire and fuse connections. Finally, test the lights and accessory for some time to ensure the housings and wiring do not become excessively hot. When I wire something on the truck, I ask myself, will this survive Hell or High Water, a Zombie Apocalypse or the *Baja 1000*?

Off-Road Lighting

Auxiliary lights are a practical modification for anyone that might find themselves traveling off-road after dark. Adequate lighting helps avoid dangerous obstacles (from bulls to boulders), that can ruin a perfectly good off-road experience.

In my youth in the mid-80's, one of my first modifications was to add six *KC Daylighters* to my *Chevy Luv* 4x4 pickup. Four across the roll bar and two up front on the brush guard.

They looked great and I still remember the first night run when I was amazed how bright they all were. Blazing down a windy forest trail, it was like driving in daylight. Then, the smell of something burning. It was the wiring and switches getting hot from not running relays.

We all get excited about something new and can overlook the directions. In off-road wiring, there are no shortcuts, or you get the privilege of using your fire extinguisher. The recent innovations in lighting and the flood LED lighting options have expanded over the last few years. Here is a review of the three different styles:

Halogen Old school, most likely your headlights are halogen. Good light output, lowest cost, lowest life span and highest power consumption.

HID Many headlights are use HID. Highest light output, higher cost, longer life span and low power consumption using a ballast. HID lights use high internal voltage in a gas filled bulb to form a high plasma to create light. They are much brighter and efficient than halogen. For example, a halogen light would be rated at 150 watts to create as much light as a 35-watt HID light. The primary advantage to HID is that they shine for the longest distance.

Hella Lights

Need to drive 100 MPH at night? HIDs shine the greatest distance.

Ford Expedition prerunner project gets a new set of 6 LED lights.

*This four LED light bar combination is ideal for
the McLaren desert race team.*

LED Most off-road lights now are LED because they are so effective, reasonably priced and have a much lower amperage draw compared to halogen or HID systems. For example, for the same luminous output, a halogen light might draw over 12 amps where the LED would only require 3, typically ¼ less. LED lights are also more shock resistant although their light output distance is less than HID.

Because watts vary so much between halogen and LED, a more accurate way to measure light output is Luminous. All lights regardless of style should have a luminous rating to them.

KC lights released some innovation in their Flex and Pro6 line of their modular LED systems that can be stacked and connected to custom lengths with a variety of beam patterns.

Driving Lights
You may have factory auxiliary lights mounted in or under your front bumper. These practical lights are great to use because they are low enough to leave on in traffic. They can easily be updated to LED options, or the factory incandescent bulb can be upgraded to become brighter. For example, many auto makers use H3 bulbs that are only 55-watt. Try a 100-watt bulb to make these factory lights more useful. Just make sure you do not pop a fuse or have oncoming drivers flash their high beams at you.

Front Lights
These are your lights to use off-road or when another vehicle is not driving towards you.

There are many combinations available for round housing lights or light bars. It is most effective for using both a spot and flood beam lights for a good balance of lighting up what is immediately in front of you as well as doing a long-range scan.

For example, two to four round flood lights or an LED light bar will make a good splash of light in front that wraps around to give you some side coverage also. This really complements the headlights well by lighting the ground in front of you as well as improving your peripheral vison. The side illumination is very helpful to avoid deer and other animals that might dart out in front of you.

For a longer-range view, possibly add two to four round spotlights that allow you to scan the horizon 100-200 meters or more. This helps spot obstacles or traffic to allow you to safely adjust your driving accordingly. Remember HID lights shine a longer distance than LED, so they might be considered for higher speed driving such as in prerunning off-road racing.

Backing Lights

Factory reverse lights are not nearly bright enough, making auxiliary backing lights very useful. LED flood lights are ideal for adding the light needed for backing up, setting up camp or hooking up trailers. The easiest way to hook these up is to tap into the existing wiring from the factory reverse lights. It is convenient to have them on their own switch allowing the lights to be turned on anytime without the need for the ignition on and the vehicle in reverse. Especially for working behind the truck and setting up camp.

Rear lights need protection and should be mounted in the bumper or up and out of the way instead of under the rear bumper.

Backing lights need protection so best mount them in the rear bumper, on the rear roofline or on a swing gate or rear rack.

Mount them anywhere to keep them up and out the way. The easy solution is bolting them on under the rear bumper, but with any off-road driving, they will soon be broken.

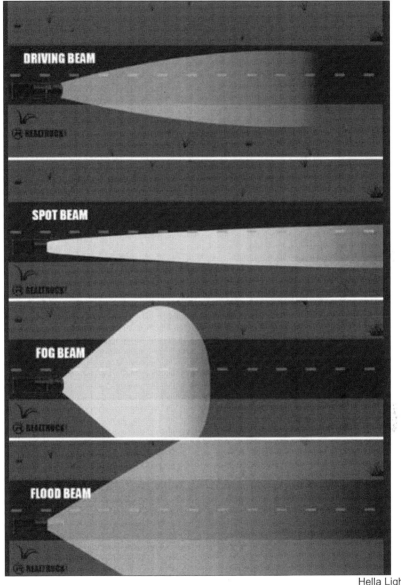

Hella Lighting

 White or Amber lights? Amber tends to work better in fog, dust and on snow.

LED Lights Still Require Using Relays

To properly wire any lights you first must understand amps. When lights or any accessory is turned on, the electrical power it uses is rated in amps. Your alternator is also rated in amps, such as a high output alternator might put out 135 amps.

My expedition-work trailer has three Hella work lights that used H3 blubs and I easily changed them out to LED replacements.

Do not throw out all your old lights yet, it can be easy to convert them to LED.

With a high output alternator and high-quality battery, you will have no problem running lights, winch and radio while the engine is running. If no engine is running, the more amps used the faster your battery will go dead.

LED lights use a quarter of the amps than halogen lights, but relays should still be used to protect the switches and wiring. For example, most light bars 40-50" use a 17 amp draw so no problem using a 20-amp relay. If you buy lights in a kit that include the wiring harness, a relay will already be included in the right size to handle the amp load.

I purchased four 51-watt LED lights for my truck and wanted to know if I operate all four on one relay. There is an easy way to find the amp draw. Take the number of watts and divide them in the number of volts (12) to determine the amp draw. For example, with my four lights, they are 51 watts each x 4 = 204 ÷ 12 = 17 amps. That means I can operate all four lights from one switch and one 20 amp rely.

Relay Wiring

Using relays is critical for high amp accessories such as off-road lights and electric fans. Relays are a switch activated by a dash switch that provides a direct fused power source to the accessory. This is a safety measure that prevents high amperage from going through and burning out the switches.

Relays have four or five numbered male connectors:

30   Fused power from battery
85   Ground
86   Dashboard switch
87   Output to accessory
87a   Output to accessory off with power load (used to turn off driving lights if high beam headlights are on)

GPS and Radios

GPS receivers and radios are straight forward to install. Two wires, positive and ground, with a coax line out for a remote antenna. The primary consideration is that you make sure it can be mounted in a way that does not block your view and it is secured to not come loose and airborne while off-road driving.

Radios with removable heads are ideal for mounting in accessible dash and overhead locations. Regardless if it is GPS screens, radios, computer tablets or cell phones, get a mount and lock them down. Shy away from suction cup or drink holder gadgets. Get mounts by companies like *Ram* that you can bolt down.

This is a Kenwood dual band radio head and Garmin GPS combo mounted up and out of the way in my Land Rover Discovery.

Ryan Blandford

GPS and radio mounted in a Chevy Colorado.

A Ram mount is ideal for locking down a 7" Garmin Dezl
GPS to the overhead console in my Ford Expedition.

RPG Off-Road makes a Lowrance mount for the Ford Raptor.

Ram makes mounts for virtually any type of electronic
device to lock them down safety in place.

Antennas

With antennas, the higher the better, but this can be a problem with
low branches. Whip base mounts help. I have had guards fabricated
to help protect antennas from tree branches.

VHF/UHF antennas operate best with a ground plane, meaning on a
metal roof as a base for the signal to bounce off from. For those not
interested in drilling 1" holes in their roof, companies like *Evil
Manufacturing* make rear brake light kits with antenna mounts in them.

*Custom antenna rack I had fabricated with room for VHF, AM/FM,
CB and GPS complete with a front tree limb guard.*

Evil Manufacturing rear brake light system complete with antenna mount with backing and pre-run lighting.

Plugging it All In and Turning it On

Carefully test each accessory to help ensure everything is wired correctly. Plan ahead, write wiring color codes down, and keep checking your work to make sure all of the wires and connections are right and securely fastened. Ask yourself, could the wire loom contact any metal and cause a short? Turn on each accessory individually and leave on for a bit to see if there are any popped fuses or excessive heat generated.

The Least You Need to Know

- Determine the accessories you plan to run so the electrical system can be built to meet the power requirement.

- Understand the options available to build or buy an adequate fuse, relay and switch panel.

- Learn the many options if off-road lighting including the pros and cons of halogen, HID and LED lights.

- Understand the importance of using a relay adequate size fuse for each high-power use accessory.

- Be sure to mount GPS receivers, radios, tablets, and phones in a way that keeps them secure for off-road driving.

- Plan the mounting of your antennas to keep them protected from tree branches.

- When wiring accessories, ask yourself, what is the weakest link? Will your work withstand whatever abuse and high water you can subject it to?

5.   TRIP PLANNING AND CONSIDERATIONS

Prepare and Pack for Success

The difference between a great trip and a disaster is as simple as being prepared. Obviously there are too many variables to plan for every possible problem, but if you cover the basics, you'll have much better odds of surviving whatever nature, man or machine throws at you.

Consider the following 'general travel advice.' We'll then get into more specific considerations for international travel including what it takes to ship your truck overseas. Also, special considerations for taking the family and traveling with children. Then, it is time to look at traveling with man's best friend.

With a little planning we can travel and live well outdoors. This is me working at my solar powered office in the Oregon Outback, 2003.

General Travel Advice

Whether traveling to well-known areas in your own state or to unknown foreign lands, there is general travel advice that will serve you well. Much of this is quite basic common sense. It is always good to review and possibly pick up on something important you may not have thought of before.

The Internet has literally put the world at our fingertips. With as much information so readily available there is no reason not to research where you want to go.

There are many clubs, organizations and even *YouTube* videos of real people doing what you want to do and where you want to go. Make the transition from being a naive tourist to an informed traveler. Do your homework and knock out one bucket list adventure at time!

 The best and most enjoyable way to travel through any unfamiliar lands is with an experienced guide and within a group seeking a similar experience or objective.

Acquire Local Knowledge

If you cannot travel with an experienced group at least consider acquiring a guide who knows their way around. If you ever get the choice between a good map or a good guide, choose the guide. Local knowledge is excellent to ensure you are going to get where you want to go and find what you are looking for once you get there. This is how to be a traveler instead of a tourist. A guide can help you discover the best places to go, play, stay and eat from a local prospective.

 Use an amateur radio or satellite phone to communicate with the outside world. Understand that your cell phone will probably not work well beyond a city's limits.

Three Ways to Communicate

Establish multiple options to communicate with the outside world as well as the ability to communicate with the locals if they speak a different language. Multiple ways to communicate can include cellular phone, satellite phone and amateur radio. Also bring along at least one person in your group who can interpret and speak the local language.

Dress for Success

Wear the right clothing to protect yourself from the elements. Packing clothing that allows you to dress in layers helps regulate yourself to the weather. A brimmed hat and long sleeve shirt will help protect your skin during the day and a heavy coat will cut back the chill at night. Also bring a large tarp to create an awning off the side of your truck. One end can be tied from your roof rack and the other propped up by a pole or with a branch. This quick shelter will keep the rain off and provide a little shade from the summer heat.

Bring Navigation Gear

Knowing your way around is critical so if traveling in unfamiliar territory be sure to bring along the right navigational gear.

Use GPS and carry all navigation tools necessary including maps, compass and a notebook.

Travel as a Group

Do not venture out by yourself or you could become one of those lonely skeletons tucked away in the back of a cave like in the movies. There is safety in numbers. Bring at least one other vehicle to give you a way out in the event of a breakdown. Better yet, connect with others of a similar interest for a group expedition. An experienced guide can also help you with details and logistics like insurance, permits, visas, knowing the local area and speaking the language.

Besides, traveling in a group can be much safer and more enjoyable. Within a group, chances are good that someone else knows how to find and get around the places you want to go. There is also an increased chance that between you and your travel mates, there will be needed parts, tools and knowledge available to fix most problems that you might encounter on the trail.

How much gear is too much or not enough? It depends on how much room you have and how much you are willing to pack around. Jason Criss did an amazing job of organizing the back of his JK.

If You Need it, Take it With You

Off-road travel is all about being self-contained. In more remote areas you will probably not find many service stations or grocery stores. The time of night you roll through town, they will be closed anyway.
You will have to take extra fuel, water, food, tools, and spare parts including at least one full sized spare tire and cooking fuel.

There is no shortage of gear that would be nice to have along, although there is usually space and weight limitations, so we cannot pack everything. Especially in Jeeps and other mid-sized vehicles where space is a premium. The trick is finding the balance between being prepared while still avoiding overload.

On-Board Gear Kits

There are full gear lists in **Appendix B**. The following is what we consider to be the very minimum, starting on the top of the list for importance.

John Miller, Lane County SAR

*Having gear in bags and backpacks is helpful
so you can take it out or take it with you.*

Regardless of how packed your truck is, you can still make room for the mission critical accessories.

My Bugout bag in Bolivia, from the 4WD to the burro. Who knows where your next adventure will take you?

Leaving an accurate travel itinerary is the single best way to help insure someone can find you if you fail to return.

Leave a Travel Itinerary

Telling someone where you are going is important no matter how many people in your group. Besides where you are going, tell them when you are leaving, how someone can contact you, and when you are planning to return. Update your plans with the outside world in the event you plan on changing your destination. See *Appendix A* for a sample Travel Itinerary.

Check the Weather Forecast

Check local weather reports before packing up the family and heading over the mountain pass. The Internet, AM radio stations, weather cable TV stations and the state's department of transportation agency are good sources for weather updates.

Camping with the crew in the walls of a private villa to protect against the banditos and smugglers outside, Sacambaya Valley, Bolivia.

Select the Best Places to Camp

Find established campsites off the main trail and away from others. Respect others privacy and need for solitude, peace and quiet. Do not camp in areas that will have a negative impact on the land, water, wildlife or historical areas.

International Travel Considerations

There is nothing quite like the adventure and challenge of traveling in a foreign or under-developed country. Does your destination include a location where you might experience crime, civil unrest, military conflict or a natural disaster? Or possibly political disturbances, kidnappings or terrorist violence?

I can't think of a location that is not subject to some kind of potential problem, so this is good advice regardless of where you are going.

What Not to Bring

If in a country where firearms are illegal, do not bring any guns or ammunition. If you need security, hire locals to do it for you. Do not bring any controlled narcotic substances that you do not possess a doctor's prescription for. You may be arrested and held in custody for possessing any amount of contraband. When in doubt, ask before bringing it. Expect you and your vehicle to be searched at will with no warrants or probable cause needed.

Driving Tips

Speed limits outside the United States are in metric, posted in kilometers per hour. An easy formula is to take the kilometers per hour posted, multiply by 6 and then drop the last digit. 100 kilometers per hour equals approximately 60 miles per hour. When in doubt, go with the flow of traffic without speeding.

Another important tip is whenever possible, drive during daylight hours. Driving at night is more dangerous than most think, with three times the fatality rate than during daylight. This is because visibility is naturally impaired and there can be a number of objects in the road that are more avoidable in daylight.

Some drivers do not use their lights, or if they do, the taillights may not work. In some areas, drunk driving is more socially acceptable. If a collision is their fault, you could still be arrested. It is also not uncommon to come across slow-moving vehicles and farm animals. You hit the cow, yes that's right, you just bought it.

Travel Advisories

Before packing your bags, keep an eye on the news, weather and if there are any special circumstances that you need to be aware of. In a world of constant unrest and changing political tides, check travel advisories with the **U.S. Consular Affairs Office, American Citizens Services** www.travel.state.gov Telephone (888) 407-4747, from outside the United States, call (202) 501-4444.

The **U.S. Department of State's Consular Information Sheets** are available for every country of the world. They describe entry requirements, currency regulations, unusual health conditions, the crime and security situation, political disturbances, areas of instability, and special information about driving and road conditions. They also provide addresses and emergency telephone numbers for U.S. embassies and consulates. See *Addendum C*.

Civil Unrest

Every country has protesters take their frustration to the streets, but some protests are more dangerous than others. Many protests are at courthouse steps or parks that can be easily avoided. These events become much more dangerous when they enter public streets subjecting unexpecting motorists to vandalism and violence.

Clarissa Claire Ramcharan

Many civil unrest protest scenes are marked with roadblocks and burning tires. If you come across this, it is time to turn around.

If you find yourself driving into a conflict that doesn't look too civil, the best thing is to immediately turn around and find a way to bypass the disturbance. If you become stuck and cannot turn around, do not stop. Roll up windows, lock the doors and keep the vehicle moving. Do not try to argue, fight or reason with protestors/rioters, must keep rolling until you can speed away. During the BLM/ANTIFA riots in the United States, 2020, multiple random bystanders we pulled from their vehicles and beaten.

If you are traveling in an area or country that is not your own, you could be a target by simply looking different. Fortunately, more serious conflict events are easy to spot by damaged vehicles, property, news media and burning tires. In Bolivia, I was surprised to hear explosives used for parties and protests.

Lisi Menkley, Daily Universe

Riots in Provo, UT attempt to stop a Ford Excursion. The driver did not stop and was still fired upon, wounding him with a handgun round. Stopping could have giving the shooter a better sight picture and allowed others to pull him from the vehicle making a bad situation potentially fatal.

Police and Military

Don't be surprised when you run across government roadblocks. In some countries it is not uncommon to be stopped by police/military personnel with automatic weapons, and then have yourself and vehicle searched. They are most likely looking for illegal weapons, drugs or other contraband which you should not have.

Police searching vehicles at a checkpoint in Mexico. In Baja, I have seen military checkpoints where soldiers were hiding along the roadside ready to pull the tire punch strip if anyone tries to run it.

Many countries like Mexico, use a Neapolitan criminal justice system, meaning you are guilty until proven innocent. Do not expect legal rights or due process that you might have in your own country.

If you encounter police, they could issue you a ticket or possibly fish around for 'mordida' payment. I have a friend who had success by asking if there was a fine they could pay to avoid going to court. Be extremely careful about this as you could be arrested for offering a bribe. Having said that, it doesn't hurt to bring gifts. In Mexico we smoothed things over with bottled water and Baja 1000 racing stickers and t-shirts.

When in doubt, ask for a violation in writing or to meet with their captain with an interpreter if needed to fully understand how to pay or dispute any violation you may be charged with. Despite your need to for protection, a firearm can get you in prison. Fortunately, carrying knives and machetes are typically acceptable. If it is serious, it may be the time to contact your country's embassy.

Health Risk and Immunization Information

For the most current information on immunizations and health risks contact Centers for Disease Control and Prevention (CDC), www.cdc.gov/travel International travelers' hotline (888) 232-3228.

Contact the World Health Organization for information about outbreaks of infectious diseases abroad, www.who.int/en and at the World Health Organization's International Travel and Health page, www.who.int/ith

Travel Itinerary

As previously stated, it is critical that you leave a detailed travel itinerary with someone at home. This is even more important traveling in foreign lands. Besides leaving the information with a loved one at home, register with your country's Department of State. Americans register at: https://travelregistration.state.gov/ibrs/ *See Appendix A*.

Once you arrive, register with your country's embassy and/or one of the local consulates. Taking the time to do so will be well worth the effort in the event of an emergency.

In areas where firearms are not permitted, lightsabers are acceptable. Just kidding, that is a full-sized sword carried by a rather intense man I met in India. Most everyone, everywhere, carries some form of knife.

Passports and Visas

Get a passport, even for domestic travel. It will expedite your border crossings and airline boarding as many U.S. state's driver's licenses are not accepted as federal ID. Passports need renewed every 10 years and can be rushed for an additional fee at an official government passport office.

If you are traveling on official government business, you should obtain a *visa* from or from the agency sponsoring your travel. Many foreign countries will also require a visa to obtain permission to cross into their border. A visa is an endorsement, or stamp, placed by a foreign country official granting permission to visit that country.

If a visa is required for your destination, make a request for one from the appropriate foreign consular representative. This requires some planning ahead to allow adequate time for your application to be processed. Processing time and fees will vary depending the country and the application method. For specific details, consult the Embassy or Consulate of the country you plan to visit.

Make extra photocopies of your travel documents including airline and hotel reservations, passports, visas, and other travel documentation. Keep these copies somewhere as safe as possible hidden in your vehicle or in a hotel safe. Also include these copies with your travel itinerary that you leave with someone at home.

Immunizations

Due to international health regulations adopted by the World Health Organization, a country may require International Certificates of Vaccination against yellow fever and/or other diseases. Prophylactic medication for malaria maybe necessary for travel to some countries.

For additional health information, contact the U.S. Centers for Disease Control and Prevention, www.cdc.gov telephone (877) 394-8747.

Shipping Vehicles Overseas

You may consider having your vehicle shipped to a destination country for the following reasons:

- It may not be possible or practical to charter expedition vehicles in the destination country.

- It will be worth the extra expense to have your own equipped vehicle(s).

- It may be simply too dangerous to drive through areas of the world needed to arrive at the destination country.

While considering shipping vehicles overseas, it is necessary to get information that can be obtained from the consulate of your destination country and from vehicle shipping companies. U.S. export requirements can be obtained from the Bureau of Industry and Security, Division of Outreach and Educational Services, telephone (202) 482-4811. Consider the following points:

- Does your destination country allow the importation of automobiles?

- What are the vehicle environmental and safety regulations?

- What are all the costs of import? Costs include custom's duties, taxes, bonds and insurance.

- Is there support for your vehicles brand? What is the availability of spare parts and mechanic services?

Other considerations for shipping vehicles and equipment:

Shipping Methods
Depending on destination country, vehicles are shipped Roll on-Roll off method, driven on and off a ship such as a ferry.
This is typically the lowest cost. The other method of shipment is by container, typically, by 20 or 40-foot steel shipping containers. This method is more expensive but provides additional room for gear and supplies as well as providing the security of having all property in a locked container.

Vehicle Shipping Preparation
Clean vehicles to expedite inspections. Fuel tanks should be low, a quarter tank for less. Non-permanent racks and longer antennas may need to be removed. Vehicles should be prepared for extreme weather and condition use appropriate for the destination country. This could include tires chains, extra electric cooling fans, proper radiator coolant and oil, etc.

Vehicle Documentation
Required documentation will include the following:

- A letter of instruction to the vehicle transport company.

- A vehicle condition report.

- Notarized copies of the vehicle title. If there is a lien holder, a letter may be required from the lien holder granting permission to transport the vehicle from its country of origin.

- A complete inventory list.

Carnets

For shipping from the United States, consider the assistance of an ATA Carnet. The United States Council for International Business (USCIB), issues and guarantees ATA Carnets, that allow temporary and duty-free imports overseas. Carnets are "Merchandise Passports" that simplify customs procedures for U.S. product shipment to 75 countries and territories.

Using the Carnet service can save considerable time and money that includes reducing paperwork and eliminating foreign value-added taxes, (VAT), duties and the posting of bonds or security that otherwise may be required. Carnets also simplify the re-entry of property into the United States by eliminating the need to register the goods with the U.S. Customs Office at the time of departure. For more information call, telephone: (866) 786-5625; (212) 703-5078, or on the web, http://www.uscib.org/index.asp?documentID=718

Traveling with Women and Children

The most remote and difficult parts of the world are still filled with women and children, so I am in no way suggesting that they are incapable of making the journey, nor would I underestimate their ability to survive once they get there.

Traveling and experiencing the world's wonders with as a group or family that includes ladies and children, I believe is always more enjoyable then traveling with the guys alone. Having said that, there are obviously potential risks to consider for anyone traveling that can especially hold true for ladies and children. Here are some special considerations:

- Middle Eastern and some countries proscribe a strict code of conduct and dress for women. It is important to learn the local customs and laws to avoid problems.

- Women traveling alone can find themselves vulnerable, possibly even breaking the law in some Middle Eastern countries.

Brooke Dannen

- It's typically best not to stand out. Leave extravagant clothing and jewelry at home. Even excessive makeup can make you a target of robbery or harassment.

- Be sure to have any needed prescribed medications with you in amounts that are adequate for your length of stay.

- Bring prescription information and keep drugs within their original containers to indicate the medication is yours.

- Be sure that your health insurance coverage will protect you internationally. If your domestic health insurance does not cover you, it may be necessary to purchase traveler's insurance.

- If you are pregnant, be sure you understand the potential complications of obtaining pre-natal or delivery care and what legal complications may arise if your child is delivered in a foreign country.

- Be aware that in remote areas, ladies will probably not have all the privacy and sanitary facilities you might like. The toilets may not flush (if you're lucky), you might have to make your own.

- Keep children close. The excitement of being in new locations can make them want to run off to explore. Children can be targets for abduction.

- Understand that children may not share your enthusiasm for long, hot, dusty trips followed by unfamiliar food. Activity books and snack foods will help keep them occupied a little longer.

- Do not have a child's first name visible on clothing or luggage, but do include a copy of contact information on the child or in their luggage in the event they become lost.

- Keep a list of emergency contact numbers that include your county's embassy, state department or consulate as well as contacts for in-country medical and legal assistance.

Traveling with Dogs
A special contribution by Jens Störmer, translated by Marcel Ae

Why take a Dog on an Extended Journey?

Unlike cats, which often prefer staying in their familiar surroundings and might not notice the departure of their usual 'can opener', dogs are used to living in packs. Nothing is more important to them then being close to their pack. At the same time, dogs are adventurous and mobile. They view the time spent in a new environment as an interesting and joyful expansion of their own territory. The owner definitely also benefits since it certainly is more fun having the dog around than worrying if Aunt Marge is actually feeding him properly.

Taking the dog along has many advantages. Goofing around at the beach for example is a lot more fun with a dog.
Their natural watchdog instincts also substantially increase camping ground security. In addition, your vacation often is the only time of the year where you have time to go hiking or even swimming with your dog. As you can see, there are numerous reasons for taking your dog with you on trips ranging from the short weekend getaway to the month-long Sahara expedition. However proper planning is necessary to make each trip successful and enjoyable for all participants.

Different Dog Characters
Most dogs like driving in cars. They love the rapid movement and watching the constantly changing landscape pass by their windows.

Christian Beck

However, this is only true for dogs that associated positive experiences with driving. It is therefore necessary to familiarize your dog with driving and visiting unfamiliar places at an early age. A dog who travels by car once a year when visiting the veterinarian will be more skeptical than dogs who know that a longer drive is usually the prelude to an extensive walk, games or the opportunity to mingle with other dogs.

There is no special training necessary for a dog to become a good globetrotter.
The only requirements are a stable character, self-confidence and the unconditional acceptance of the master's decisions and commands. Take your dog to a puppy school so that he can learn these things and how to cope with unusual sounds and environments as well as how to properly interact with other animals and humans.

Some dogs are better-suited for certain destinations than others. A city tour for example can cause extreme stress for an anxious dog. Dogs that tend to beg or are eager for attention can cause problems in restaurants or when traveling with larger groups. Just keep in mind that not everyone out there is a dog lover.

Health Considerations

If your dog is healthy, he will be able to bear all the challenges you see yourself capable of handling. Usually dogs can endure a lot more than their adventurous master. However, one should take the age of the dog and potential cardiovascular problems into account when planning a trip in hot areas. Black dogs as well as dogs with dense fur should not be exposed to intense sunshine, since this increases the risk of heat stroke or circulatory collapse. Dogs with joint problems (hip dysplasia, arthritis, etc.) on the other hand might feel severe pain in cold weather, which is why you should refrain from taking them on winter trips.

Remember to take your veterinarian's phone number with you. It might come in handy in case of an emergency. Tip: Veterinarians have a very practical surgical device that temporarily mends bleeding wounds. You might want to ask your veterinarian if you could borrow this device for the trip or even consider buying it. In any case, your veterinarian should explain the proper use of the device. Start preemptive treatment against fleas and ticks early. Also, while on the trip, keep your dog away from wild dogs as they might have contagious diseases, flees or other parasites.

Before You Hit the Road

Check the entry restrictions of each country you plan to visit well before you embark. Good sources of information are automobile associations, national tourist offices or embassies. You should make yourself aware of all restrictions that may apply to traveling with dogs e.g. in national parks, restaurants, hotels, places of interest, etc. Not every country is as animal-friendly as you might expect.

Visiting your veterinarian well in advance of the trip is also very important, as it is crucial that the dog's vaccinations and respective records are up to date.
Several countries require a federal veterinarian's certificate. In some Arabic countries this needs to be translated into the local language. Terminate all plans if the country requires quarantining your dog. No trip is worth inflicting the mental stress of quarantine on your dog. Also, ask your veterinarian for a list of drugs and their proper doses for emergency situations.

Where to Place the Dog While Driving?

Your dog needs sufficient space and standing room even if space might be limited due to luggage and other equipment.

A non-slip surface is crucial. Most dogs will also appreciate a blanket to facilitate nest building. Make sure that there are no sharp edges close to the dogs that might cause injuries.

You should also consider installing a heavy-duty safety net between the front and the back of the car's interior. Please be especially careful when storing equipment in areas close to your dog. Also, monitor the flow of air from your air conditioning. Dogs can easily catch ophthalmitis or otitis when exposed to substantial drafts for prolonged periods of time. Special breathers fixed to the ceiling are a good way to minimize drafts within the car. However, they might reduce the resale value of a car.

One way of keeping the car's interior cool is to mount a large board on or beneath the car's roof rack. This reduces the sun's direct impact as it creates a constant shadow for the entire car. It might also be helpful to tint the car's rear windows. If possible, try using specially treated foil which reduces UV radiation but at the same time only slightly impacts overall visibility.

Ferries and Boats

You might want to skip the dog's last regular meal and take him for an extensive walk before boarding a ferry. Once on board you should look for a quiet place in order to avoid adding the additional excitement of other people, sounds and animals to this unfamiliar situation. In no case should you leave the dog on the car deck as high temperatures and increased CO_2 levels create an unhealthy environment.

Ferry companies often require dogs to be locked up in small boxes on the main deck which lack any kind of weather protection. This is not the right way to treat a dog as it can get rather cold at sea at night depending on the season. As long as your dog is able to remain quiet you should take him into your cabin, if you have one. Objecting cabin personnel can usually be "persuaded" with a generous tip.

Off-Road Driving With Your Dog

Off-road driving is very challenging for every dog. He has to offset the car's rapid and unpredictable movements by balancing his own weight. In order to help your dog adjust, you should allow him to get accustomed to off-road driving by starting him off with easier excursions. Dogs usually feel most comfortable if they are able to push themselves against a cushioned area of the car.

If provided with appropriate space in the car, an experienced dog certainly is capable of mastering this feat in very rugged terrain.

Still you should avoid jumps, abrupt stops, etc., and try to keep the trip as smooth as possible. In addition, you should allow your dog ample time to get into his position before entering a rugged area. It might even be worthwhile to teach him a special command.

Camping in the wilderness – where should the dog sleep?
Choosing whether the dog should sleep inside the car, outside of the car or even in the tent depends on his race and character. The same holds true for the question if the dog should be kept on a leash or not. Over time we personally have come to the following conclusion: We sleep in a tent on the roof of our car while the dog rests in his familiar spot in the car. We leave the vehicle's backdoor open so that he can independently take care of any pressing needs.

Please consider the fact that your dog might detect a cat or a rabbit during the night. Keeping him tied on a regular leash could cause serious problems. Collars are inappropriate, harnesses are a better choice. We have had success with a Husky racing harness combined with a long, slightly-elastic, mountain rope. These harnesses are custom made by specialized companies and therefore are suitable for all larger dogs. To reduce the risk of the leash getting entangled overnight, you should consider removing tables, chairs, and all other equipment from the dog's potential path.

Since 1989 Jens and Sabine Störmer have conducted several camping and off-road trips with their dogs throughout Europe and northern Africa. They share their house with a Doberman and a Jack Russel Terrier mix.

 Pack trash bags to carry your garbage and any other debris left behind by someone else. We should leave every environment better than how we found it.

The Least You Need to Know

- Follow good travel advice whether on expedition at home or abroad. This includes traveling with a group with the experience to help ensure a successful trip.

- Successful trips require doing your homework. From packing the right gear, clothing and what you need to communicate and navigate.

- When traveling overseas, be sure to check current travel advisories. Also, register with your countries' state department once you arrive for added measure of security.

- If transporting vehicles or supplies overseas is necessary, do your homework to help ensure trouble-free shipping.

- Understand the potential complications such as privacy and venerability for traveling women and children.

- Dogs provide extra security and companionship but may be not as easy to get into or out of foreign counties as you might think.

6. OFF-ROAD DRIVING

Let's get Down to the Business of Driving

The greatest factor in off-road driving is not so much the vehicle or equipment, but the knowledge of the driver. Our own driving ability is the greatest asset, or liability, we have when it comes to getting through the rough stuff safely.

Because off-road driving can be dangerous and cause vehicle damage, it is critical the driver maintains control and drives in and over terrain that is within their comfort and experience level. Like any other skill our proficiency and confidence increases with practice and experience.

A great way of learning off-road driving is through a class. I had the privilege of attending a training program by Camel Trophy participant, Bill Burke of 4-Wheel America.

Turning off the Pavement

There is a list of considerations when you are ready to abandon the security of asphalt for the thrill of dirt path least taken. Here are some practical things to consider getting you and your truck home shaken but not stirred.

Read the Instructions

Believe it or not, the owner's manual is full of useful information. Check it out to familiarize yourself with useful information such as the vehicle's four-wheel drive system and jacking points. This will be especially helpful if the truck is equipped with higher-tech electronic or automatic four-wheel drive and differential locker systems.

 Pump the brakes Ivan Stewart. Don't turn into the mud yet without knowing how to put your truck into 4WD Low. You are going to have to stop, put it in neutral, and practice the 4WL transfer before you need it.

Give Yourself Enough Time

Off-road travel means slower driving and everything taking longer than you think. Any repairs and recoveries required can take hours. Be sure you budget enough time and daylight to do it right.

Get Everyone on the Same Channel

Do not rely on cellular phone coverage in remote areas. Agree on a radio frequency everyone can tune into for CB, Family Radio Service or amateur radio. VHF Amateur Radio is preferred because it provides the best communication within the group as well as being strong enough to contact the outside world. (See Chapter 16 Communications)

Top 'Er Off

Check your fuel level and double-check your calculation on how much fuel you'll burn to the next fuel-up point. Remember you will use more fuel per off-road mile than driving on pavement.

Last Minute Inspection

Do a walk around and take a final look to be sure your truck is up to the task. Frequently check fuel, oil and fluid levels. Your vehicle is your lifeline back to civilization so check it over before, during and after off-road use. Look closely for leaks, wear and damage. Catching a problem early will give you more options in dealing with it.

Pack it Right

Balance your gear so the heaviest is low and to the rear, such as fuel, water, ice chest, propane tanks and stove. Save the lightest gear such as folding chairs, shovel, axe and bedding for the roof rack. Be sure that tools, jack and recovery gear are easily accessible. If you are stuck or have a flat tire off-camber, you will not want to dig through your other baggage to find what you need.

Be sure all cargo, supplies are tools are strapped down and secured. A dog guard works well to separate the rear cargo area from the back seat. Cargo can become airborne during a crash causing serious injury or damage.

Air Down Tires

Airing down tires improves traction by widening the tire's footprint for better ground control. Airing down also softens the ride to help reduce vibration over long washboard tracks. Try different pressure levels depending on the terrain. Try 20 pounds for dirt, gravel or hard packed roads. Be willing to go down as low as 12 to 15 pounds for deep sand, mud and snow.

Use extra caution when driving with low tire pressure for three important reasons: Sharp turning maneuvers can break the tire's bead, causing the tire to roll off the wheel. Reduced air pressure reduces the tire's height, reducing overall ground clearance. And finally, driving with force over sharp or abrupt objects such as rocks can cause damage to wheels.

Buckle Up & Listen Up

Use your seatbelt and consider five-point racing belts if traveling at high speeds. Also, turn off the stereo and fans so you can hear what is going on around you.

 Understanding your truck's physical dimensions will help prevent damage. The larger the vehicle, the more susceptible it will be to overhang dragging and trail rash.

Know your Clearance, Angles and Size

Understand your trucks stance before hitting the rough stuff. Being conscious of this information helps reduce body damage by knowing the size of obstacles you can safely drive up, over and through. Know how much ground clearance you have on your lowest points being at the axle differentials. To help dodge obstacles, know if your differentials are centered on the axle or offset.

Also, know the most vulnerable parts such as front air dams, rear overhang, bumpers, side mirrors and exhaust. The best way to protect the vehicle is to understand its overall physical size. Typically, the passenger side of the vehicle gets the beating. Keep in mind your width, length and height when traversing down twisty mountain trails.

Besides ground clearance and dimensions, you need to know your approach, departure angles and break-over angles.

Know your angles and clearance before you hear that scraping sound.

The approach angle runs from the bottom of the front tire up to the lowest front body piece, usually an air dam or bumper. The departure angle runs from the bottom of your rear tire up to the lower body piece, usually the bumper and exhaust. The break-over angle runs from the bottom of each tire up to the mid-center of your frame and drivetrain.

Remember Your Off-Road Access Trail Head

Unless you are planning a point-to-point trip, you'll want to remember your access point to return to after your off-road run. This is a good time to save the turn off as a GPS waypoint as well as reset or start a track log you can keep a record of your tracks electronically (see Chapters on using GPS).

Shift Into Four-Wheel Drive

It's always a good idea to go ahead and shift into four-wheel drive before you get stuck. A common rule is if you are in an area that is too rough to drive a regular car, go ahead to shift into four-wheel drive. Getting outside the truck to switch to manual locking front hubs is always easier when you are not up to your knees in muck.

Use 4WD high range if driving on hard packed terrain. Shift down to 4WD low range if driving in deep mud, sand, snow or steep terrain. This is important because if you need the power and torque of low range gears, you will most likely not have time to shift your transfer case down into low range once you have committed to driving through, or over, a challenging obstacle.

Based upon your speed and ground conditions, shift into four-wheel drive before you need it! Remember 4 low range will probably require stopping the vehicle and putting the transmission into natural first.

Getting Down to the Business of Off-Road Driving

You feel your heart beating in anticipation of the freedom and excitement of traveling over remote roads only a select few have followed before you. Adrenaline flows and every sense is hyper-aware as the rumble of tires rolling over terrain and obstacles you didn't know you could so easily conquer. It is time to get to the skills that make this possible.

Driver Position
Sit up straight or lean over the steering wheel for a better view. Upcoming terrain can be difficult to see by looking over the hood. Get a better view of the immediate ground by watching the front tire through the side window.

Put your passenger to work as a spotter by having them watch what is going on up front, or better yet, kick him out to spot in technical sections. Use extreme caution when sticking your head outside of a moving vehicle as branches and other obstacles provide a serious hazard, especially if your truck shifts or slides out of control.

How Fast is Fast Enough?
Smooth is fast. It is momentum that rolls a truck though the most challenging terrain such as soft sand or deep mud. An increased speed will help you motor through obstacles, although going too fast can result in getting stuck further, losing control and inflicting vehicle damage. If your tires begin to spin, back off the throttle until you regain traction. Most driving experts agree you should drive fast enough to get through without driving any faster than necessary.

The bottom line, driving too slowly can cause you to bog down and get stuck from losing your momentum. Drive too fast and you risk losing control. Find the right balance to get the job done depending on what kind of terrain you are traversing. Desert racers will agree that for racing or pre-running, covering ground quickly means picking the right track lines and driving smoothly and consistently.

The faster you drive while crashing or becoming stuck, the worse off you will most likely be. Drive all out fast all the time, and sooner or later (probably sooner), you will be the guy upside down.

Let your eyes follow the trail about 25 meters ahead. This will make for a smoother ride as you will have time to pick the best line and negotiate around hazards.

Picking a Line

Motorcycle riders often make the best off-road divers because they understand how to pick a line. They know that getting their front wheel in the wrong track and they are ass-over-tea kettle. Most non-paved roads form into a double-track. Tire tracks from four-wheeled vehicles eventually wear two tracks in the ground. Over time the grooves become deeper causing a hump to form in the middle. The grooves become deeper in muddy conditions forming to hard ruts when the ground dries again. These tire grooves can also become washboard or form a series of larger bumps known as whoop-de-doos. Other hazards include rocks and boulders that turn up within the tire grooves.

As the driver, your job is to pick the best line which is simply the smoothest and safest route. Most of the time that means driving within the naturally formed tire grooves in the dirt road. If they become too rutted or bumpy, try driving up and out of the grooves to one side or the other. Use caution by reducing speed and looking for obstacles when making the transition in and out of the tire grooves. Forcing tires out of grooved ruts at speed can cause damage to steering components and tires, as well as easily cause the loss of control.

Simply taking the exact line as the guy in front of you may not be appropriate considering possible differences in width, driver skill, tires and ground clearance.

The analogy of a double-track road. Depending on how deep the ruts and other conditions, you can drive in the groove or on top of it.

 For automatic transmissions, practice using your left foot for breaking. This allows you to navigate off-road obstacles by feathering the throttle and brake at the same time.

Driving as smooth as possible is all about picking the right line. Sometimes you are in the rut groove or on top of it. Other roads are just too washed out to matter.

The more twisted the ground get, the more fun it is to drive.

Transmission Considerations

Auto Use your left foot to brake to allow your right foot to remain on the accelerator. Most moderate off-road driving will be done in 2nd or 3rd gear with the transfer case in low range. Shift down if you start to bog down, shift up if your tires are spinning.

If stopped on any kind of angle, use your parking brake. Do not rely on using your transmission park mode to support your vehicle alone.

Manual Also use your left foot to brake. Do not drag or ride the pedal. Keep your foot off the clutch pedal until needed. Most moderate off-road driving will be done in 3rd gear with the transfer case in low range. Shift down if you start to bog down, shift up if your tires are spinning.

If you stall in a difficult driving situation where pressing the clutch may cause you to roll, you may be able to start the motor without using the clutch. If your vehicle requires the clutch to be pressed to start, use your parking brake and press the clutch lever down just enough to allow the engine to start, then ease off the parking brake while applying the throttle.

Throttle Control

Throttle action should be smooth and steady. When working in technical areas 'bump' the throttle to power through or over obstacles. If your tires are spinning, back off the throttle until they regain traction. Spinning tires will typically only dig you in deeper instead of propelling you forward. If tires are spinning frequently due to excessive torque, shift up to the next highest gear.

Rest the throttle foot against the transmission tunnel (left hand drive) or right inner sidewall (right hand drive). This will help stabilize your foot on the accelerator during bumpy driving.

 Do not ride your brakes. Doing so may cause them to overheat and fade. Shift down to let the engine compression slow your vehicle.

Brake Control

Typically, the less use of the brakes the better. If you need to reduce speed, come off the throttle and shift down, allowing engine compression slow you down (especially on long declines). If you approach an obstacle that you need to slow down for, apply your brakes to do so before reaching it. If hitting a bump or rock, release the brake to allow your wheels to continue to roll, allowing your suspension to fully cycle.

Do not ride the brakes. Doing so may cause them to overheat and fade. If you need to reduce speed, tap the brakes just hard enough without locking them up. If you need to come to a complete stop immediately, smoothly, yet firmly apply the brakes until stopped. Again, if possible, avoid locking up the brakes to the point of skidding or sliding.

ABS computer braking systems can take longer to stop a vehicle, but the tradeoff is they can prevent wheel lock-up, skidding and sliding. Unfortunately, ARB systems do not always work well during off-road driving conditions, resulting in even greater stopping times and distance. Many off-road drivers install a switch or pull the fuse to disable ABS while off-road.

Steering Control

Drive with hands at three and nine o'clock on the steering wheel. Keep your thumbs outside of the steering wheel. This will protect your thumbs if the wheel jerks out of control. Most steering inputs should be smooth with just enough turn as necessary. Over-steering or erratic wheel movements may cause the need to counter-steer, increasing the chance of becoming out of control.

Always be conscious of what direction your front wheels are pointing. This is especially true when driving in heavily rutted areas where the vehicle can abruptly pull off-course once the tires break free. If tires are lodged in ruts, do not force them to turn while stationary. Forcing tires to turn (especially with the hydraulic force of power steering) can cause serious steering component damage. If you feel as though you are becoming stuck, steering the front wheels in a back-and-forth in a zip-zag pattern can help regain traction.

Steering components such as the tie rod are probably the easiest to damage. You've bent it if you find that your steering wheel is turned to one side while driving straight.

 Off-road driving is all about being smooth and staying in control. Good driving practices rarely involve heavy or erratic throttle, steering or brakes.

Maintain Control

The key to safe driving is maintaining control of the vehicle at all times. This means slowing down, driving smoothly and going light on steering and brakes. If the driver controls the truck, they can decide the direction and speed of travel.

Erratic driving with sudden throttle, brake and steering controls can cause an undesired shift in the vehicles center of gravity potentially causing a collision or roll-over. Once control is lost, the vehicle bounds under the uncertain direction of gravity, momentum and fate. Lots of off-road driving advice can be summed up in a few favorite quotes:

"**Drive with Finesse**." After some practice, you can develop your own style. A primary key to this is driving ahead of yourself. The driver needs to think and drive in both short range and long range at the same time. Scanning the trail ahead 20 to 40 meters (depending on speed). Seeing potential obstacles ahead of time allows you to drive smoother and faster by responding to the terrain instead of reacting to hazards.

"**Drive as Slow as Possible but as Fast as Necessary**." Good advice. Going slow prevents damage, but sometimes going faster prevents getting stuck. Keeping momentum is the key.

"**Good Off-Road Diving Rarely Requires Drama**." This is true, but there is a certain guilty pleasure in spinning and sliding tires in dirt and splashing through muddy water. At least be conscious of not driving irresponsibly and do not drive in a way that damages the environment.

As stated by professional driver, Doug Shipman, "*95% is Behind the Wheel*." Too many of us depend on our accessories to get us through. The space between our ears is our greatest asset-or in some cases our worst enemy. We need to control what we do and were we go."

Get Out and Have a Look
Not all off-road driving is from behind the wheel. When in doubt, get out and have a look up close and personal. Walk obstacles through to pick the best route. This gives you the opportunity to see rocks, stumps and other potential hazards hidden under water, mud, snow or grass.

Apply Common Sense With a Good Dose of Caution
Do not drive outside your comfort level. Be realistic about the limits of both your vehicle and your driving ability. If obstacles look too difficult for either, there are options, such as backing out to find another route. You can also ask another driver of a greater skill level for assistance.

 Be courteous, friendly and helpful to those you meet on the trail regardless of their form of travel. Maintain good Karma because you never know when you might have to ask for help.

Good Off-Road Driving Practices

These are tried and true practices for safe and successful off-road excursions.

Travel in a Group

Plan your remote outings as group activity or at the very minimum, go with at least one other vehicle. Traveling in a group is not only more enjoyable, it is also best for security and safety. Another good reason is if there is a breakdown, the odds will be greater there will be the knowledge and hopefully the spare part will be available within your group to keep everyone rolling.

Before hitting the trail, decide what radio channel will be used for group communications. Assign a *Tail Gunner* to take the rear as a sweep. This is the best way to ensure no one gets left behind.

Keep Your Distance, But Keep Them in Sight

When following other vehicles, maintain enough distance that will allow the truck ahead to stop or even back up. This may be necessary when the driver ahead of you is trying to negotiate technical obstacles or back out of a wrong turn and especially important when climbing hills. Leave enough distance that if the driver fails the hill climb, they can back up and try again without rolling into you.

When following another driver, watch and learn from them. Essentially, you will have to decide to take their line or drive an alternative path.

While maintaining a safe travel distance, keep in visual contact with the truck ahead and behind you. Follow a convoy rule that after making a turn, wait until you see the vehicle behind you in your rear-view mirror before proceeding. Use caution about stopping in a blind cover to prevent the driving from hitting you. Keeping an eye on the guy behind you will go a long way to help prevent anyone from getting left behind or lost by taking the wrong turn. Use a Tail Gunner sweep vehicle in the rear with a radio to ensure everyone is accounted for.

Drive with Preservation in Mind

Not only for the environment, but also for the rig you expect to take you home. If your truck is not designed for racing and jumping, don't drive it like you're in the *Baja 1000*. Take care to protect your tires, engine, drivetrain and the many other parts and systems all needed to get you home without a tow truck.

Use a Spotter

If in a potentially difficult situation, do not be afraid to ask for a spotter. Use someone with experience that you trust to give good advice. Agree in advance about hand signals because vehicle noise may prevent verbal communication. On the trail, *no*, *go* and *whoa* all sound the same. If necessary, use a spotter for both the front and rear of the truck. Remember however, that more than one person can provide conflicting advice.

Brett Cifaldi

This is an ideal place to have a spotter. Steep inclines and drop offs make it is difficult for the driver can see what they are getting into.

Do Not Drink and Drive

Sounds obvious, but some are under the impression that it's OK if you're driving off-road. Not true. Off-road driving requires more concentration that driving on pavement. Any amount of alcohol or mood modifying substance will negatively affect how you drive. Save your drink for the end of day campfire, but know that being hung over will diminish your driving ability.

Back on the Pavement

Once again, do a careful walk around inspection of for leaks and damage. Air tires back up and check fluid levels. Clean off mud thoroughly to avoid rust. Depending on the type of excursion, some servicing may be in order such as changing the oil and cleaning the air filter, etc.

The Least You Need to Know

- Give your rig a good inspection before and after off-road excursions.

- Airing down tires to about 12-16 pounds of pressure greatly increases traction in all off-road driving conditions.

- Understanding your truck's physical dimensions and its off-road capabilities will go a long way to prevent vehicle damage.

- Good off-road driving requires smooth and light usage of throttle, brakes and steering.

- Drive as slow as possible but as fast as necessary.

- Never travel alone. Going with at least one other vehicle gives you an alternative way back. Traveling in a group provides additional expertise to solve most repairs and problems.

- Avoid damage and getting stuck by kicking your passenger out to spot you through technical obstacles.

7. OFF-ROAD OBSTACLES

Hold On, Things are Going to Get Rocky

Congratulations, you and your beloved truck and getting the hang of off-road driving and with confidence building, you are daring to go where most never will. Hills, water, mud, rocks and other obstacles will be tackled in no time after a little homework and practice.

Covered in dirt and a grin from ear-to-ear, it's time to get beyond the basics to discover the fun and challenge of driving off-road obstacles. Shift your transfer case and transmission into low range and let's get going.

 Put your vehicle in 4WD before tackling difficult terrain. Once committed to the challenge, you will not want to break your momentum to stop and shift your transfer case.

 Understand your driving abilities and vehicle limitations before tackling any technical off-road driving. If needed, find another driver or route.

Hills

Maneuvering up and down slopes is one of the most common and potentially dangerous off-road challenges. Depending on the grade, may require a little planning to get up and over safely.

Scott Turnbull

The tricky part about climbing is you cannot see what's in front of you.

111

Going Up

Hills should be tackled as straight up and down as possible to help prevent a possible roll over situation. Manual or automatic transmission, you are going to have to pick a gear and stick with it. This requires staring with the transfer case in low range.

Steep inclines will not allow you to reduce momentum by taking time to shift in mid-climb. A gear too low may only spin your tires and not allow you enough speed to get over the top. A gear too high may not provide the low-end power necessary to get over the top. For example, with a manual transmission, with the transfer case in low-range, try second or third gear.

Often the tops of hills are heavily rutted due to previous failed or full throttle climbs in muddy conditions.

Bruce McCallum

This requires picking a line carefully to find the smoothest route. Do not let up off the throttle until you are safely on top, then over the hill. Stalling near the top can result in a very difficult and sometimes dangerous exercise in backing down. Only after successfully completing the climb, then back off on the throttle and reduce speed to prevent going down the backside of the hill too quickly.

If you are not sure what the backside of the hill looks like, it is best to hike up and have a look. This will prevent you from blasting over the top to a steep drop off. Walking up to the top also provides an opportunity to check for rough spots like ruts and rocks. This is also the time to find anchors to potentially attach a winch line to in the event you must winch your way to the top.

Do not allow someone else to follow anyone climbing a hill too closely. Give the vehicle in front plenty of room in the event they fail the climb and need to back down. This also includes not parking too close to incline or decline of a hill climb in progress.

 Understand your vehicle's gravity characteristics and avoid any driving style or obstacles that could result in tipping over.

Arne and Pam Beckman

Going Down

Point your truck downhill and be sure your front wheels are straight before making the decent. Do not over steer to prevent the truck from swerving out of control. Place the transmission in a lower gear using engine compression to maintain a slow steady speed.

Use your brakes only if required, but do not let them overheat. This is done by feathering the brakes and letting off when possible to let them cool down. Remember the vehicle will stay in control better and the suspension will work to its fullest capacity if the wheels are turning instead of skidding.

Engines with carburetors could stall under extreme climbing conditions from the fuel bowl becoming flooded or starved of fuel. Fuel injected engines have pressurized fuel systems to prevent this issue.

 Engine braking is done by down shifting into a low gear, utilizing the engine's compression to slow the vehicle down. This works with a manual or auto transmission and is ideal to avoid overuse of the brakes.

Ricky David

Failed Hill Climb

One of the most difficult off-road challenges is recovering from a failed hill climb. If your truck fails to make it to the top, there are some quick decisions to be made. One option is to back down as carefully as possible for a faster run to try it again. Before doing this make sure the next person in line has not gotten too close behind you. There is also the options of winching to the top or having a lead vehicle pull you up with a tow strap.

Jans Stoermer

To make matters more ominous, being stuck on a steep incline can be a little intimidating. Your truck could be sliding downhill, and the view limited to nothing but sky through the windshield. Furthermore, accelerating to the point of wheel spin can cause you to only dig in deeper or result in the truck shifting out of control. You should not try to turn around, as turning the truck on an incline can result in rolling over. If winching or using a tow strap for a pull up the top is not an option, you will have to back down.

Donald Perez

To do so, stop to stabilize the truck. Place the transmission in reverse.

Place your driver's side hand on top of the steering wheel and your passenger side hand on the passenger seat headrest. This allows you to physically turn your body to look behind you through the rear window. While in reverse let the engine compression allow you to make a very slow and controlled descent, only braking as necessary.

Overuse of the brakes will limit steering and suspension travel. Be sure to back straight down and remember that steering will be sensitive, meaning smaller steering inputs can cause the truck's rear wheels to dart out of control. If your truck begins to skid, carefully and easily apply some throttle and turn into the direction the rear of the vehicle is moving.

If you stall your engine before the crest of the hill, firmly use your footbrake to keep from rolling. Do not use your hand brake if it locks the transmission instead of the wheels (like with *Land Rover*). With your foot on the brake, start the engine and continue to ease down in reverse. A stalled engine with an automatic transmission will not provide compression braking. If you have a manual transmission, you may be able to re-start the engine without the use of the clutch.

 Failing to make a hill climb and having to back down is probably one of the most potentially dangerous off-road driving situations. Back down slow and straight to prevent a possible roll over.

 Do not follow a vehicle climbing a hill too closely in the event they fail the climb and need to back down.

Side Hill Slopes

It is always best to approach sloped ground straight up or down, but on occasion you may find yourself driving on side slopes. If you must, do not drive at such an angle that will result in rolling over. Stay within a 35-degree angle without exceeding 45 degrees. Use extra caution if your vehicle is loaded with gear. The weight should be carried as low as possible and in extreme cases, remove gear from a roof rack and kick out the passengers to reduce the chances of sliding or tipping.

Get out and walk the slope to help ensure it can be safely traversed. Pick your line of travel noting any obstacles on the uphill side or holes on the downhill side that will increase the angle of the slope. Shift your transfer case into low range and only drive as fast as necessary to get through. If your vehicle begins to tip or slide, keep your wheels straight and stay off the brakes while you drive through it. If the slope becomes worse, roll to a stop to reassess your route.

If you must travel through a steep slope, consider digging a trench for the uphill side tires to reduce the angle.

 Use extra caution driving on side slopes if a loaded roof rack and other gear makes your truck top heavy.

 Do not try to turn around on a steep hillside. If you fail a climb, you will have to winch or get towed up or back down.

 Hill Descent Control **uses ABS to maintain vehicle control on hills and slopes, although the same driving techniques apply.**

Donald Perez

Remember in off-road travel, any hills you drive down,
you may have to drive up for a return trip.

Obstacles

What makes off-road driving as fun as it is challenging is to improve your skills to see what you can make it through. On the trail, you may not know what you will encounter next, but with practice, you will be bumping and wheeling through the rough stuff with the best of them.

Mud, Sand and Soft Terrain

The trick to driving in soft terrain is finding the line of least resistance to maintain forward momentum without getting stuck. This requires always knowing what direction your front tires are pointing and maintain an adequate rate of speed.

Knowing where your tires are pointing is important considering it takes less energy to propel your truck forward than negotiating tight turns. If you must turn around, a larger turning radius will provide less resistance to reduce the chance of getting bogged down.

Maintaining enough speed is also critical. Driving through soft sand, mud or snow is all about pushing through without getting stuck. Driving too slow can break the momentum causing you to bog down or the engine to stall.

 Before trying to tackle off-road obstacles, understand your vehicle's low points, limitations and just how big of an obstacle your truck and driving ability can take.

Ricky David

118

Going through deep mud? Don't stop or slow down.
Off-road driver Martha Tansy shows us how it's done.

Keep applying throttle, steady and smooth until you can power your way through. If tires start to spin, you may be digging down instead of propelling yourself forward. If this happens, back off the throttle enough to allow the tires to regain traction. If loosing traction, apply more throttle and try turning the steering wheel back and forth quickly in a seesaw fashion. This may help the front tires to dig into firmer ground to regain traction.

Often muddy conditions require negotiating deep ruts. This can be a technical exercise as you decide to drive in, on, or over ruts. If driving in ruts, be cautious of where your front wheels are pointing. The ruts may guide you in their direction regardless of where you are pointing the steering wheel. Once out the ruts, the vehicle could abruptly jerk to one side if your steering wheel is sharply turned.

Power steering components can also be damaged if forcing wheels to turn while stuck in deep grooves or ruts.

Ravines and Trenches

Dirt roads often wash out creating ravines that cut across the road or a deep "V" groove down the center. The procedure is the same for crossing any long obstacle such as a trench, crack in the ground or log.

Approach the obstacle at about a 45-degree angle, allowing you to drive over one tire at a time.

This allows three tires on more stable ground while one drops in or drives up and over the obstacle. Approaching obstacles at an angle prevents both front tires from sinking into or bashing into what you are trying to cross. It also prevents becoming high-centered or dragging the vehicle's rear overhang.

 When driving over logs be extra careful not to run tires over broken branch spurs as they can easily puncture tires.

You may find the entire road is washed out resulting in a large trench. This requires picking a line where the tires straddle the trench. If the trench is wider than the vehicle, this requires driving on the tire's outer sidewalls. Proceed slowly, keeping the vehicle as level as possible. Doing so will help avoid sliding or rolling. If the vehicle starts to tilt or slide, carefully turn into that direction and apply additional power to level and stabilize the truck.

Rocks

Often dirt roads are washed and weathered away leaving boulders in the path. Use the tires to roll slowly and carefully, directly over rocks and other obstacles. Doing so raises the entire vehicle, maintaining ground clearance.

Climb obstacles using the tire's tread, taking extra precautions not to damage and scrape the tire's much more vulnerable sidewalls. Also take caution not to damage your vehicle by slamming into or down from protruding rocks. Try not to straddle rocks, as they easily get hung up and damage drive train and other undercarriage components.

If you must pass through an area with a protruding boulder, incline/decline angles can be eased by using dirt and rocks to build a ramp before and after the obstacle. If possible, roll over larger rocks on the driver's side. Most flats are from hitting rocks and obstacles with the rear passenger side tire. In tight technical areas, it's always best to hug the driver's side to help prevent damage to the passenger side.

 Have your passenger get out as a spotter while traversing any difficult obstacles. Having another set of eyes on the ground is critical for preventing damage and making better driving decisions.

Donald Perez

In boulder fields and other technical areas, get your passenger out to spot for you. Have them be your eyes on the ground and under the truck to help you select the best route through. Both driver and spotter need to be aware of the lowest and most vulnerable areas of the vehicle. This includes tire sidewalls, steering rods, axle differentials, the exhaust system and rear overhang.

 Be prepared to re-track your route If you believe the terrain ahead is unsafe to cross.

Water Crossing

Crossing waterways is referred to as *Fording*. If you are planning on taking your truck through water, plan ahead to help prevent serious mechanical and electrical damage. Before you drive through any flow of water, get out and check how deep it is and the bottom conditions. Walk through the crossing area with a walking stick to check for water depth and swiftness.

Crossing water that is too deep or moving too swiftly can wash your truck away. Look and feel for boulders, logs, deep ruts and other obstacles that could hidden by flowing water. It is critical that water does not draw into the air intake system. Doing so will fill the engine's cylinders causing the motor to seize.

Ronny Dahl

If this happens and your engine stalls, you can attempt to dry it out once recovered from the water. Remove the spark plugs and turn the motor over to help cycle the water out. Check to see if water has entered the engine's crankcase. If your engine has taken in any amount of water, the chances are very good that it is damaged far beyond what you can repair on the trail.

The best way to prevent water in the engine is to extend the height of the air intake system with the use of a snorkel. Besides keeping the water out, snorkels also provide a benefit of drawing colder and usually cleaner outside air. Water can also leak into differentials, the transmissions, the transfer case and the fuel tank. The most likely entry for water to leak in are the breather ports. Consider running a breather line up into the engine compartment or even up the snorkel.

Besides the engine and drivetrain, electronics must be protected. Run a silicone bead of sealer around the distributor cap, spark plug wire ends and electronic boxes such as the fuse box and the vehicle's CPU computer box. Electronic plugs can be better sealed with marine grease. Consider sealing the CPU box in its own plastic protective container or getting a wire plug extension allowing the box to be relocated in the vehicle's cab.

Donald Perez

When crossing, drive through at established crossing areas. This may provide a more stable underwater path across the river and help prevent damage to natural waterways.

Cross flowing streams at an angle, pointing slightly upstream. Drive just fast enough to maintain the momentum to carry you through. A moderate speed will create a front bow wake. Driving too fast will only splash more water up into electronics and air intakes.

Crossing water over the depth of the bumper only increases the chances of water damaging the engine or electronics. Use extreme caution if getting into water levels reaching your headlights. Consider placing a tarp in front of the radiator. This may help prevent the fan from spraying water over the ignition and electrical components. Once out of the water, drag your brakes for a moment to dry them out. After deep or extended water crossings, check to be sure water has not entered your truck's oil cases.

 Getting out and physically checking the water depth is critical. If the streambed dips, this may submerge your vehicle to unsafe levels resulting in water damage.

 Do not drive down a streambed or drive in a way that would cause damage to the natural waterway and wildlife environment.

It always looks tempting to drive through the surf, but remember that saltwater will destroy electronics instantly.

If You Stall

Once engaged in technical driving, do not shut off the engine unless you are going to stop for an extended period of time. Considering erratic driving conditions with water and mud, it is not unusual for an engine to stall. With an automatic transmission, apply the foot brake, then the hand brake to place the transmission into park to restart.

For a manual transmission, apply the foot brake, then the hand brake. This frees up the foot brake for the clutch and accelerator pedal. Another procedure is to apply the foot brake and shift the transmission in to first or reverse. Then turn over the ignition without depressing the clutch. The starter will propel the truck forward, then ease off the foot brake as the engine starts.

Applying the brakes is important, because if on an incline, you should not rely on the transmission alone to hold the vehicle in place.

The Least You Need to Know

• Understand the limitations of your vehicle and driving experience before tackling more advanced off-road driving.

• Shift your transfer case into four-wheel drive before you need to. You will not want to break your momentum to stop and shift once committed to driving a technical obstacle.

- You will probably not have time to shift during steep hill climbs. Shift transfer case into low and pick a transmission gear that will get you up and over.

- Give yourself plenty of room between vehicles in the event the truck in front needs to back down or out of an obstacle.

- Most long obstacles are best crossed at a 45-degree angle to allow better traction with three tires on more stable ground.

- Get through soft terrain by picking the best line and powering through. Spinning tires only bury you instead of propelling forward.

- Prevent damage by negotiating rocks by carefully driving over the top of them instead of straddling them.

- Kick your passenger out of the truck and put them to work as a spotter for traversing more technical terrain.

- Get out and walk through any water crossing before driving. Underwater holes can submerge your truck to damaging levels.

8. DESERT CONDITIONS

Where the Streets Have No Name.

Blazing heat during the day and piercing wind with bone chilling temperatures at night, nothing will kick your butt like the desert. With harsh sun and little shade, why would anyone in their right mind want to venture out in such an unrelenting environment?

To adventurers it's only natural to want to challenge ourselves and machines in the planet's most extreme environments. Besides the desert has always been a place to lose our way but find ourselves on the journey. The natural beauty is enough to take our breath away. Getting up early enough to witness a desert sunrise can be nothing short of a spiritual experience.

Jan Stoermer

Remote desert travel is all about being totally self-reliant. Water, food, fuel, tools and parts, you are required to carrying everything needed to travel overland and camp in different locations for both man and machine. Desert travel requires a minimum of two trucks in the event one of vehicles becoming stuck or disabled.

 Driving in sand requires going as fast as necessary to maintain momentum to prevent getting stuck, then not stopping until you hit solid-flat ground.

Maintain Momentum

Sand and silt suck up serious horsepower. When you feel the truck bogging down, smoothly accelerate and use momentum to get you through loose terrain. Be careful not to spin your tires, this will only cause you to dig in further. Using a higher gear may prevent spinning. Try 4WD high in drive, 2nd or 3rd gear with a manual transmission. Maintain enough speed to allow you to use momentum to get you though without going too fast. Excess speed causes damage by losing control or hitting rocks and obstacles harder that you would like.

Christian Beck

Pick Your Line

Desert travel off an improved road involves double-track driving. These roads are tire grooves with a buildup of rocks and vegetation in the center. To prevent damage to your vehicle and the desert environment, it is important to stay on the road or trail the best you can. This typically means driving in the grooves or trying to stay up and out of them. If the road is smooth, but made up of soft sand, driving in the groove may or may not provide better traction.

The ground is more firmly packed in the groove or it may be more stable on the crest. Check it out and drive where your truck feels the most stable. If the terrain is varied and the grooves are deep, stay out of them. Chances are that whoever made the tire grooves has larger tires than you do, or floodwater has cut them deeper. These can cause your truck to be pulled out of control or high-centered on the center mound.

Maintain Control

Go easy on the steering and brakes. Sharp turns only cause the tires to dig in and bog you down. Sharp turns and sliding can also cause aired-down tires to roll off the bead. Using the brakes can cause sand mounds in front of your tires, another obstacle to overcome when taking off again. The sand will usually cause you to slow down quickly by just letting off the throttle.

Desert driving is usually the fastest form of off-road driving. While it's great fun to bomb down open desert roads, it can be easy to lose control. If you need to slow down fast, lightly pump the brakes without causing the tires to skid. Do not lock up your brakes while going over rocks or bumps. This will cause your tires to skid and limit your suspension travel. The idea is to reduce your speed before the object, then allow your tires to roll over it.

 Sharp turns can break the bead on air-downed tires, rolling them off the rim. Larger radius turns also provide less tire resistance to help from being stuck.

Watch for Rocks

Desert roads are often littered with outcroppings of large rocks and boulders. It is not uncommon to run across microwave oven-sized rocks right in the tire groves even on the smoothest of desert double-tracks. Slamming rocks is the best way to cause serious havoc like blown tires and bent tie rods. Know the unprotected areas under your truck. The differentials are the lowest point of ground clearance. Do you know where your differentials are? On most *Rovers* they are off-set to the passenger side.

Donald Perez

Watch for Floodwater

When it rains in the desert, dry ditches and riverbeds can quickly turn into flash flood zones. Get to higher ground and do not drive through floodwater without knowing what the terrain is like underneath. Watch out for driving over dried lakebed crust that contains mud underneath. This condition can get your truck hopelessly stuck.

These conditions are known to exist in such areas as the *Black Rock Desert* in Northern Nevada.

 In countries like Mexico, hitting and killing livestock can get you arrested. Either way, it going to cause damage and cost money.

Watch for Livestock

Many desert areas are open ranges with herds of cattle camped out on the road just around the next blind corner. Open range livestock and wild deer are a practical reason to have an aftermarket front bumper. Needless to say, crashing into a 1,200-pound bull will ruin your day and his. Besides totaling your truck, you may have to buy the beast to compensate the rancher for his loss.

 Airing down tires can double your traction by allowing the tires to float on top of the sand.

Airing Down Tires

Good tires are critical for driving across silt and sand. The idea with loose terrain is to drive on top of it instead of digging into it. This makes a wider all-terrain tire a better pick than a narrow mud-terrain style. Reducing tire pressure down to 12 to 16 pounds will greatly improve traction by widening the tire's footprint. You just need to be extra careful driving to protect your tires' sidewalls. Do not slide into rocks, and if you can't avoid obstacles, roll over them with the tire's tread instead of glancing off it with the less durable sidewall.

Stop on Firm Ground

Even long desert roads must come to an end. If you must stop in loose terrain, wait until you are on stable hard-packed ground or at least pointing slightly downhill to allow you to get going again.

Use your AC

Rolling up your windows and turning on your air conditioner will help keep the dust out and give you a little cleaner air to breathe.

Ed Sandman

The Least you Need to Know

- Being self-sufficient is critical for desert travel. If you need it, you better take it with you.

- Never travel across the desert alone. It is best to have at least two vehicles in the event one is disabled.

- Desert driving requires going fast enough to maintain momentum and powering through soft sand without spinning.

- Maintain control by going light on the steering and brakes.

- Don't stop driving until you have reached flat solid ground.

- Airing down tires can double your traction by allowing the tires to float on top of the sand.

9. WINTER CONDITIONS

Staying on the Road Means Staying in Control.

Have you ever taken your family to play in the snow? Everything is going great until your truck is doing a 360-degree spin on a mountain road in traffic. A terrible feeling comes over you when you realize that you have lost control of your truck as the blurred scenery swirls in front of you. I must admit this has happened to me and after my heart stopped pounding, I promised myself I would take the time to learn how to prevent this potentially fatal experience from happening again.

Even the mighty H1 Hummer is not immune to getting stuck. This truck was recovered on a late-night mountain SAR mission.

Winter driving sometimes turns into winter sliding, because it is easy to make mistakes, like not slowing down. Driving in the snow can be great fun, but it is also an auto body shop owner's favorite season for a reason. A responsible winter driver will take the initiative to learn how to drive in the worst conditions to make your snow-bound trips safer ones.

 Remember four-wheel drive improves traction not so much steering and braking.

Slow Down

Reduce speed before contact with snow or ice. In freezing temperatures, approach wet surfaces carefully as it may be black ice. Once on snow or ice it is critical to drive as smooth as possible, staying in control by going light with the accelerator, steering and on the brakes.

Remember back in driver's education when the instructor said drive as though you have an egg between your foot and the accelerator? This is good advice when driving on snow or ice. Any sudden or abrupt acceleration, steering or braking can quickly cause your vehicle to slide.

Studs or Chains?

Tires are one of the biggest issues when it comes to winter driving and tire chains provide substantial improvement for traction and braking. Chain up before driving on packed snow. The *National Safety Council* conducted a test on an ice-covered course in Wisconsin. They found that snow tires offer a 28% improvement over a standard tire. Studs provided a 183% improvement, but chains provided an impressive 630% improvement over standard tires.

 If you have only one set of chains, put them on the front. It is your tires that best control the steering and braking.

Ryan Burks, SVG SAR Team

Test Your Chains Before You Need Them

Be sure to carry chains with you during winter months. If you have only one set, use them up front. This will assist in steering and braking. Using a rubber mat with proper winter clothing will make the task of putting on chains more bearable. When chaining-up, do not jack up or crawl underneath your truck.

If on a roadway, do not position your body where an out of control motorist can slide into you. The best place to install chains is in a parking area away from the roadway. The best time to install them is before you get into deep or slushy snow. Be sure to test your chains in your nice warm and dry driveway before you need them. Check for fit and how many rubber bungee cords are needed to keep them tight. Some chains need to be trimmed to prevent flapping links. Throwing a chain can cause serious damage to brake lines and body panels.

 Put chains on in a safe clear location to prevent from being hit by an out of control driver.

Maintain your Momentum

Driving through snow can feel similar to mud or sand. Use enough throttle to smoothly power through areas when necessary.

Just like driving though other loose terrain, use momentum to push the vehicle through and to prevent you from becoming stuck.

Pamela Petroff, Pacific Coast Rover Club

Snow and Ice Travel

Driving slowly and giving yourself extra distance for stopping is the key to snow and ice driving. Once you realize an obstacle in front of you is too close, the normal reaction to firmly apply the brakes. Doing so can quickly cause your vehicle to skid and slide out of control.

If you have time, trying using engine compression to slow down by gently shifting into a lower gear. If you do need to apply your brakes, do so smoothly, applying constant pressure. Do not pump the brakes, instead apply steady and constant as hard as necessary without locking up the wheels. Slamming your brakes will most likely only cause you to slide out of control.

Steering out of tire tracks into fresh snow can help reduce speed. Plowing virgin snow can slow you down quickly, but turning out of tire tracks too quickly can easily put your truck into a spin.

In a worst-case scenario, you can try to select what you hit depending on your creative sliding abilities. A nice soft snowbank is a better option than the car in front of you and definitely a better option than sliding into oncoming traffic.

Ryan Burks, Special Vehicles Group SAR Team
*Special Vehicles Group SAR Team on mission in near
blizzard condition in the Oregon mountains.*

The Least You Need to Know

- 4WD's help with traction, but it does not help with steering or braking.

- Slow down! Most accidents happen when people attempt to drive their normal speed, then suddenly realize that they cannot turn or stop.

- Do not become over-confidant using chains. You can still get stuck using chains on all four wheels.

- Stay in control and on the road. Sliding off the road is all bad. The options are usually a deep snow-filled ditch, a guardrail, or a cliff.

- Do not tailgate. Remember your stopping distance will be considerably longer.

- Reduce your speed before entering potential icy areas such as shaded patches or bridges.

- Snow can hide obstacles like ditches, rocks and logs.

- Keep a close eye on other drivers. They are most likely tense, nervous, and trying to drive just like they normally would in good weather.

- Do not go alone, travel with two or more vehicles whenever possible.

- Traveling on primary roads will help you from becoming stranded. Be sure to tell someone where you are going and the route you plan to take!

10. RECOVERY TECHNIQUES

Getting Unstuck With Driving Techniques and Tools

You know that sinking feeling you get when you have sunk? Your wheels are spinning but you are not moving. That driving mistake has you on the wrong line or into mud that's just a little too deep. The motor has put out all it has, but your truck will still not budge.

Before you call a tow company (you are probably too far out for your cell phone to work anyway), take heart. There are more ways than you might think to get out of the thick of it when things look their worst. Here are several options, even without using a winch, to get you out of the hole and back before dinner. Let's look at getting unstuck by using our heads, driving skills and low-tech tools.

Gordon Kallio

Driving

Know Your Limits!

"You don't have to get out of trouble you don't get into." The quote is from motivational speaker *Zig Ziglar*, but it sounds like he was talking about off-road driving to me. Because off-road driving is potentially dangerous (to you and your truck), it is important to know your limits. Take the time to learn how to drive and invest in the truck and gear needed to get where you want to go and back safely.

Stuck without a winch? There are over a dozen techniques to try to get you home on time. The biggest tip is to not drive into anything you are unsure about.

Shift Into 4WD First!

Remember that prevention is everything. One of the best ways to keep from getting stuck in the first place is to engage four-wheel drive before you need it. Once you get stuck, it is cumbersome and sometimes potentially hazardous to engage four-wheel drive if your truck is lodged in a vicarious position.

Get in the Right Gear

In the midst of the slippery stuff, you will probably not have time to easily shift from 4WD high to 4WD low. Doing so may cause you to have to stop, which is the last thing you want to do in the middle of a hill climb. In the rough stuff, consider driving in low range and using a higher gear. That way you always have the lower gears accessible when needed.

Momentum is Your Friend

One of the best ways to keep from getting stuck is to keep moving. Don't drive too fast but be sure you're using enough throttle to get you through without bogging down.

 Off-road drivers use the term 'bump the throttle.' This is stepping on the throttle but in a controlled way. It is applying enough horsepower to break through.

Rock and Roll

One of the easiest ways to get out quick is to drive the truck back and forth to build up enough momentum to drive out either forward or in reverse. Use a rhythm to driving forward to and backward, just go easy on the drive train to avoid breaking a U-joint.

It is surprising how many times when you cannot drive forward, you can still move in reverse. This gives you hope you can still keep moving. Back up and give the throttle a good bump to see if you can carefully power through the obstacle. Quickly driving front and back can take a little practice with an automatic or manual transmission.

Go Straight to Go Forward

Make sure your wheels are not cranked too far to one way. Your truck will have less resistance to move forward with the front wheels pointing straight ahead.

Eric Gwaltney

Air Down

It's amazing how much traction is improved my letting some air out of the tires. Doing so dramatically improves your truck's footing by widening and lengthening your tire's footprint.

Airing down can allow you to drive or float on top of loose terrain like mud, snow and sand. Next time you lose traction, take the air down to 10-12 lbs of pressure. Some drivers use even less depending on the circumstances. Just drive carefully without sharp turns to avoid rolling a tire off the bead. Also remember that airing down reduces ground clearance.

 You will be amazed how much more traction you will have after airing-down your tires. Especially in sand and snow. Just be careful not to turn to sharply and risk rolling the tire off the wheel bead.

No Spinning Allowed

Once your tires are spinning, you are probably digging down instead of going forward. Try backing off the throttle to help regain traction.

Keep it Running!

If you do get stuck (especially in mud or water), keep the motor running. A stalled motor only adds insult to injury if you are already stuck.

Back to Nature

If your wheels are spinning, stop and have a look to see what you can put in front of or under them. Rocks and branches work well to give your tires something to bite into.

Pick Your Line

Let your eyes drive a little ahead of yourself to help pick the best line of travel. This will help you stay on better ground. Remember vegetation and rocks usually provide better traction that mud.

Line in the Sand

When driving in loose sand, stop on level ground or pointing at a slight downhill slope. This will help get you moving again.

Tools

High lift jacks have lots of uses. In this case, the rear of the truck is being lifted to place rocks and branches under the tires.

Get Your Shovel

Sometimes you may just have to dig out. It does not take much build up in front of tires or differentials to keep you stationary.

Use your shovel to clear the terrain from the front of your path before just spinning your way down deeper.

Up the creek without a shovel? What no shovel, haven't you learned by now to take one with you? Shovels can fold up small and have more uses that you might think. From digging a latrine to smacking down bandits, pack this essential tool. If you don't have one, it's time to improvise. Things that can be used include a license plate or tote box lid. I once used a lid from an ammo can toolbox. Even a floor mat can be used for sweeping snow or sand.

Jack it Up!

Lifting your truck is an effective way to get unstuck by the ability to place rocks, wood, dirt and branches under the tires for traction. This is critical if you are high-centered by your drive train resting on the terrain.

A Jack Mate attachment to a high lift jack provides an attachment point for a chain to making it easier for the jack to be used as a winch.

Use a High Lift Jack

Yes, they are cumbersome to carry, but when you need one, you need one. Besides, do you really think you are going to change your tire in the mud with one of those wimpy scissor jacks? With three feet of travel and 6,000 lbs. of lift, these jacks can do amazing things besides help you change a tire. They can be used like a winch to pull your truck. These jacks can also be used similar to a "jaws of life" device to opening up crushed vehicle cabs.

 Never use your ball hitch to attach your tow strap. If the ball breaks off, you just created a 2" cannon ball.

Travis Rutherford

Tow straps are amazingly strong because they are made to flex instead of break. They are more effective and safer than steel chain.

Tow Straps Required

Your recovery kit should include two tow straps, a main strap that is 30 feet long and at least three inches wide. Use a shorter strap about eight feet long as a tree trunk protector. A short strap is also helpful for attaching to two front or rear pull points to equalize the load. Use quality screw type D ring shackles to attach two straps. Do not buy or use tow straps with built in hooks.

 Do not use chain to pull out a vehicle unless there is no other choice. Unlike chain, tow straps flex. Breaking chain flying through the air can be dangerous.

Have Good Front and Rear Pull Points

Properly installed pull points are critical for recovery. Trailer hitch balls do not count. They can break off and turn into cannon balls. For the rear, use a heavy-duty D ring style that goes into the 2-inch receiver.

Bring Ladders

Sand ladders are not for everyone, but if you are doing any extensive driving in sand, don't leave home without them. Besides looking cool on your roof rack, they work great to bridge the way over soft terrain or ditches. You can make your own with strips of expanded metal or carpet.

Havas-Sarban, Sand Ladders.net

Sand ladders are easy to carry aboard and work great to get out of most stuck situations. Besides they look more professional than the rubber floor mats I had to use once.

LightWay ladders have an innovative high lift jack base built in. This is ideal for using the jack in mud, sand and snow.

A Come-A-Long Might Work

A poor man's winch might just give you enough pull to break out to freedom. They are small enough to include in your gear and not too expensive to buy. One rated for two tons, (4,000 lbs) is around $40.

Even if using a winch in the front, these can be helpful for pulling a vehicle to the side to avoid a damaging obstacle.

Chain Up

If driving on snow or ice, chain up before you get stuck. It may sound a bit strange, but snow chains also work to get through mud.

Use a Spotter

You don't want to go alone anyway. Put that passenger to use by kicking them out of the nice warm and dry cab to see what's going on outside. When trying to maneuver out of awkward positions, it is often difficult to see what is going on from the driver's seat. Having a spotter is great way to know how to back up, straighten the wheels and power out to firmer ground without damaging your truck.

Pack Sand

Wet sand provides much better traction. If there is a water source nearby, wet down the sand in front of your tires. If you are driving on a beach, do not go near saltwater, it will fry your electrical system upon contact.

Passenger Power!

When in doubt, you can always kick all the passengers out and have them push. Pushing can work best when shifting from forward to reverse and back to forward. Have your human power participants get into a rhythm of moving vehicle forward and backwards until you are moving enough to break free.

If after all these tricks, you still find yourself hopelessly stuck? Experts agree to stay with your vehicle. Not only does it make it easier to find you, but your vehicle is also your shelter as well as providing some temperature control through heat and AC.

Of course, there are always exceptions to staying in your vehicle, like if there are residences or a major intersection nearby. Remember that if you are lost in, search & rescue will be looking for your vehicle which will be easier to find than you wondering in the wilderness.

The Least You Need to Know

- A primary factor in not getting stuck can be prevented by learning to not dive over your head or abilities.

- Momentum is your friend. Drive just fast enough to power through obstacles without bogging down.

- If you can't drive forward, you can still typically move in reverse. Keep the vehicle moving forward and backward until you work yourself free.

- Airing down tires will dramatically improve traction.

- High lift jacks have multiple uses from jacking up stuck tires to placing traction material under them to being used as a winch.

- Shovels and sand ladders are low-cost tools that usually work.

- When all else fails, get your people out to push!

- If you are stranded, your chances of being found improve if you stay with your vehicle.

II. RECOVERY WITH A WINCH

Getting Unstuck With a Winch.

So you followed all of this good advice in the previous chapter and you are still stuck up to your doors in mud? When nothing else works and no one is around to pull you out, sometimes you just need to rescue yourself. Winches can be a lifesaver, but there are definitely safety considerations. Let me show you how to use a winch successfully and safely.

Mike, Pacific Coast Rover Club

After a few off-road outings the circumstances are inevitable. Even with careful driving, you proceed to place your truck in a vicarious position, wheels spinning, stomach turning, and your pride and joy is seriously stuck or potentially teetering on the brink of disaster.

From the previous chapter, you remember to air down tires, using a tow strap and placing rocks and branches under with tires with the aid of a high-lift jack. All this work and still stuck? Sounds like it's time to get serious as you discover there are times when it will take none other than a winch to set you free.

Having a winch in the front of your truck is a little like having insurance. It's not something that you need to use every day, but when your need it, you need it. As beneficial as using a winch is, they can also be very hazardous to operate.

In fact, the chances are probably greater of getting hurt using a winch that any other aspect of off-road driving and recovery. Take the time to learn how to use a winch effectively and safely before you need it.

Steve Schoenfeilder, Warn Industries

The Basics

The general rule is that you purchase a winch that is rated for double your vehicle's weight. The most common sizes are a pulling capacity of 8,000 and 10,000 pounds.

A winch recovery often requires a bit of planning. Take your time to develop a feasible plan for a safe recovery without causing damage to you, your vehicle, or the environment. Sometimes a recovery may be as straight forward as a tug to break a vehicle free, or a somewhat complex feat of engineering with multiple vehicles and snatch blocks. Either way, come up with a plan and follow through for a safe recovery.

Using a winch requires the use of strong, frame-mounted pull points. Ideally a heavy-duty D-shackle block that attach in the rear two-inch towing receiver or using two pull points that are part of a heavy front bumper bolted to the frame. Pull points must absolutely be strong enough to support the weight of the vehicle with the jerking and strain that a winch or tow strap recovery produces.

 Include a Snatch Block in your recovery kit. Using one will double the winches' pulling power and is useful when you need to change the angle of the pull.

One of the primary issues of a winch recovery is what to anchor to. Typically, this involves another vehicle, a tree, or a boulder. If anchoring to another vehicle, sometimes that vehicle also needs to be anchored to prevent it from sliding. This is why it is important that off-road trucks have both front and rear pull points. Park your vehicle square to the direction you are winching. This will assist in the cable winding properly on the drum.

Warn Industries

The winch cable runs through the block and around the pully. The block is then closed and a D shackle is inserted through the rings.

Using a snatch block when needed to change the angle of the pull.

A snatch block pulley doubles the pulling power.

They do make the winch operate a little slower but the payoff is that they double the pulling capacity, relieving much of the strain from the winch motor. A snatch block also allows you to change the pulling angle like when the anchor is around a corner.

Safety

One of the most dangerous aspects of using a winch is dealing with wire rope. Check the cable to ensure that it is not frayed, pinched, or damaged. Wire rope retains energy, meaning that when it breaks, it snaps and flies creating a hazard to anyone nearby.

Deadened the wire cable by placing some form of heavy fabric over it can help. This is often sandbags, tow strap, coat or floor mat. The idea is that if the rope breaks, the added weight will drop the cable safely to the ground.

When using a snatch block, never stand inside the deadly 'V.'
In this case if the block, D shackle or tree strap broke, the man
in the white cap would be struck with a flying winch cable.

Wire rope can easily fray causing injury to your hands, like wire steel splinters. Never operate a winch without using durable leather gloves. Winch gloves are designed to have heavy leather palms with a loose collar around the wrist that allow you to pull them off quickly in the event they become caught. If you even think you might be using a winch, keep your gloves with you so you do not have to worry about trying to find them later.

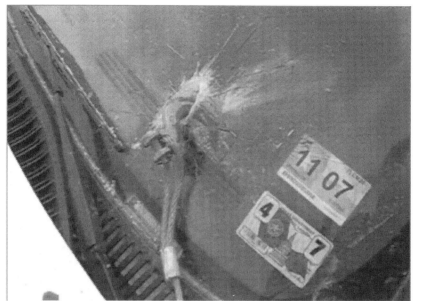

BANGShift.com

When winch tackle breaks, steel cable and hooks fly.

 Do not get fingers or gloved hands near the fairlead roller head. The power of the spool could suck your hands right in and crush them!

When handling the cable, even with gloved hands, do not let it slide through your hands. Pass the cable through hand-over-hand. Do not let your hands or anything else get close to the winch's fairlead roller head. Do not get near a cable under load. Do not cross a taut cable and if you need to cross a cable on the ground, step on it to prevent it from snapping up between your legs.

 Carry a pair of leather gloves in the leg cargo pockets of your dominate hand. Once you get in the habit of doing so, you will appreciate always knowing where they are.

Remember that if your recovery point breaks, it too will be flying through the air causing a serious hazard. Do not ever attach a winch cable or tow strap to a hitch ball. If it breaks, you have just created a small but deadly cannon ball.

When using a snatch block, never get into the deadly 'V' arc area. If the snatch block, or any of its rigging should fail, the cable will snap straight, taking out anything in its path. A winch operator can run the winch from the driver's seat. The windshield provides an extra level of protection in the event of a broken cable.

153

Members of the Pacific Coast Rover Club
had Camel Trophy participant, Bill Burke provide a weekend
of specialized training in Oregon's Tillamook Forest.

 When using a snatch block, never get your body in the middle of the deadly 'V.' If the rigging breaks, the cable can hit you with enough force to cause serious injury.

Anchor Time

Beach and desert environments may not provide much to tie onto for getting unstuck. Consider using a land anchor like a *Pull Pal*, that is designed to dig in loose ground for winching. You can set up your own land anchor by burying a spare tire in the sand and attaching the winch line to it.

Spool Neatly

Maintaining line tension while powering the cable in keeps the rope spooling neatly layer-after-layer. After the recovery, tension is applied for powering in by passing the cable hand-over-gloved hand as you guide it on the spool. Allowing the rope to spool too quickly or loosely will cause it to go haywire into a tangled mess. A tangled spool can jam the winch to the point where it is inoperable. It can also cause serious damage to the cable.

If the winch spool becomes tangled, stop winding in. Spool out enough cable to clear the tangle, then proceed to spool the rest of the cable under tension. Remember do not allow your gloved hands to get any closer than about three feet from the fairlead rollers.

During a vehicle recovery, it is not practical to stop the operation to re-spool the wire into neat rows. The wire does not have to wind perfect as long as it does not tangle. After a winch operation and once you are off the trail, it is a good idea to spool out the used cable and wind it back neatly.

 Switch the steel cable to synthetic rope. It's just as strong with half the weight, and if it breaks, it will not hold energy to fly. You can tie it together with a knot and keep going!

Warn Industries

Most winchers are changing their winch line to synthetic rope. The Fairlead needs changes also from roller to Hawes style.

Signals

Excellent communication is needed during a recovery. Turn off the radio, heater fan and roll down your windows so you can hear what is going on. Often with the sound of motors and the winch drum turning, it is difficult to hear directions. Do not use terms like "whoa"- it might sound like no or go. There are a set of hand signals that are important to learn and use for clear communication.

Here are the basics:
- Twirling finger in the air: Power In
- Twirling finger pointing down: Power Out
- Forward fist: Stop
- Fingers and thumb in a pinching motion: Tap the power to take up the slack

| Power In | Power Out | Stop |

*Steve Schoenfeilder from Warn Industries demonstrates
the three most common hand signals.*

 **Have your group or club understand and use common
winching hand signals. Voice commands are not effective
over noisy engines and winch motors.**

*Ryan Burks and the team from Special Vehicles Group remove a large
log with one of their Jeeps. Notice the jacket on the line for safety.*

Tips

- A winch recovery is a serious task that should not be rushed. Take your time to develop and carry out a plan.

- Winches are ideal for self-recovery for those times that you happen to be by yourself.

- When anchoring to trees, always use a tree protector strap and place it as low to the ground as possible. Tree straps are also great for attaching each end to two front pull points to disperse the load evenly.

- One person should be in command of the operation. Keep everyone else back and out of the way.

- A winch is at its greatest pulling power when spooled nearly all the way out. Do not operate the winch however, without at least five wraps on the drum.

- When a vehicle is being winched and breaks free, it is only natural for the driver to want to drive the rest of the way out. This risk however, when the driver over runs the speed of the spooling winch, the line becomes slack and tangles. Often it is best to allow the winch to do the work with only minimal assistance from the vehicle's own power.

- Listen to the sound of the electric motor. Due to gearing, a winch loses a slight amount of power every time a new layer of cable is spooled on the drum. The motor may have a slightly different sound as more cable is taken in.

- Pay attention if the motor sounds like it is overheating or ready to stall. If the cable is very taut and makes a 'pinging' sound, this may be an indication that it is getting over-stressed.

- Considering a winch can be potentially dangerous and somewhat technical, have your group or club conduct a training session at least one day a year. Even old winch hands will enjoy going over the basics and sharing their knowledge.

 Do not walk over a winch line. If it goes taunt, it could snap you hard between legs!

During Search & Rescue training, we tried to get trucks stuck in sand pits on the beach to practice winching them out.

The Least You Need to Know

- When nothing else will work, a winch usually will.

- Use a winch that is close to double the weight rating of your vehicle. Most are 8,000 to 10,000 pounds.

- A Snatch Block will double the capacity of your winch.

- Using a winch can be extremely dangerous. Take the time to learn proper safety techniques.

- Have your group or club understand and use standard winch control hand signals.

- Learn to re-spool winch line correctly so it's good to go next time you need it.

- Using synthetic winch line is not only safer, it is half the weight.

12. COMPASS AND COORDINATES

Learn Old School Navigation Before Going High-Tech

I must confess that my sense of direction is terrible. Maybe, it is because I want to enjoy the outdoors without paying attention to where I am going. Either way, I need all the navigational help I can get. No question about the fact that GPS changed the way everyone navigates. Once you use GPS you do not want to use anything else.

We are covering old school navigation first for two important reasons. First is GPS is still based upon navigation principles and terminology so understanding navigation will allow you to use GPS much more effectively. Second, GPS is an electronic machine that can fail, so having a backup always makes sense.

Caveman Basics

We are going to start with the very basics. Even without a compass, you can still find your way around with what nature can tell you. Remember the basics: the sun rises in the East, moves to the South, then sets in the West. At night, find the North Star, also the points on a crest moon point south.

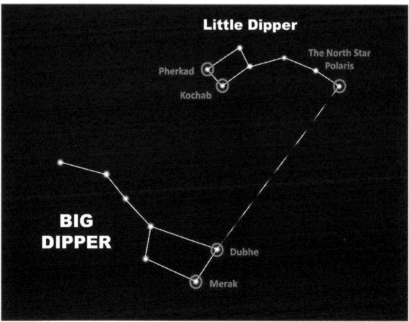

Watch the Sky

The North Star is located by finding the Big and Little Dippers.

Another navigational aid is *Terrain Association*. This is making a map in your head by referencing the landmark features you can see. For example, you are traveling north through a valley with a mountain to the East and a river to the West.

Navigational Tools

Compass
Bring at least one. The main compass should be a good quality, preferably Orienteering style.

Maps
General road maps to find the destination then topographic maps once you get there. Be sure to bring enough topo maps to cover your entire area of travel.

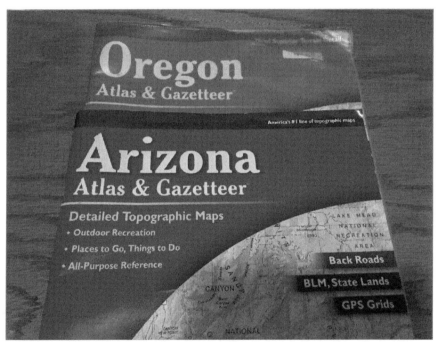

As far as carrying maps, these detailed Atlas & Gazetteer's are great.

Map Accessories
A map ruler for measuring coordinates on a paper map. A map cover protects maps, especially in bad weather. A grease pencil can be used to write on the cover.

Notepad and Pencil
Taking notes is a great way to back up navigation equipment as well as help remember the interesting points on a trip.

Wristwatch

Keeping track of time is an important navigational tool.

Using a Compass

Now that you know how to drive, let us make sure you are heading in the right direction. Learning to use a compass is the basis of navigation whether you are using a GPS or not. And you might ask, if we are using GPS, do you still need a compass? Yes, for two reasons. The compass is an ideal backup for GPS and GPS does not give accurate directional compass information if you traveling less than four mph.

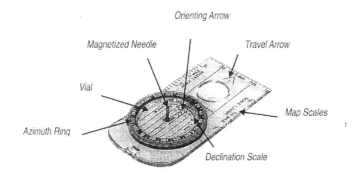

Orienting Arrow

Magnetized Needle

Travel Arrow

Vial

Map Scales

Azimuth Ring

Declination Scale

Brunton Company

The anatomy of an orienteering compass. Note the Azimuth Ring or Bezel includes 0-360 degrees with the N, E, W & S cardinal points.

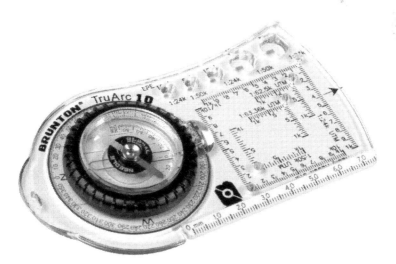

The Brunton TruArc is one of my favorites because it includes UTM map rulers and a glow in the dark bezel.

Using a compass is fun and easy once you take the time to learn how to use one. You know that needle points North, but here is where it gets a little technical. Hard to believe, but there are three variations of North.

True North Direction to the actual North Pole.

Magnetic North Direction of compass needle as it points to Magnetic North.

Grid North Vertical map grid lines that may deviate from true north. (Usually not enough difference to consider)

The two norths we are going to reference are *True North* and *Magnetic North*. This is because the earth's magnetic poles shift over time and depending on your location on the earth there will be a slight difference between true north and magnetic north.

The earth's magnetic poles do not line up exactly with the earth's North and South Poles. The magnetic North Pole is offset and its location varies over time. Due to magnetic north and true north not being the same, compass degrees require adjustment to make up the difference. This difference is called *Declination*. There is an imaginary line that vertically circles the globe known as the *Agonic Line*. Only at this line is magnetic north and true north the same.

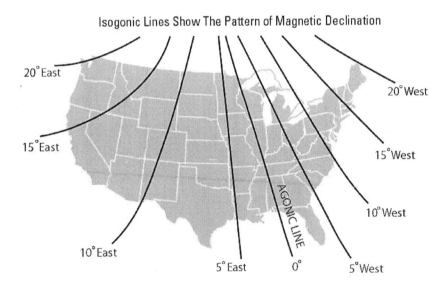

Isogonic Lines Show The Pattern of Magnetic Declination

USGS

US map showing the difference in Declination from True North.

Finding the declination for your area is easy. Your receiver will tell you in the Setup menu by selecting True and Magnetic North. Another way is to check the declination scale at the bottom on you map.

In the United States, the Agonic Line runs through Wisconsin, Illinois and Alabama. To the west of this line, the declination is to the east, requiring degrees of declination to be increased. To the east, the declination is to the west, requiring degrees to be subtracted. For example, declination in Oregon averages 18° east. Eighteen degrees needs to be added to any magnetic needle bearing to convert it to a True North bearing.

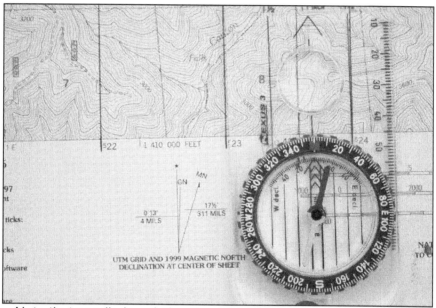

Note that needle is pointing the same degree as indicated on the magnetic north declination scale to the left. In the field it's a good idea to orientate the map to north so the map is facing the correct direction.

The above declination diagram is from a 7.5-minute topographic map of the *Bohemia Mining District*, south of Cottage Grove, Oregon. The vertical line topped with the star is true north. The line topped with GN is grid north and the line to the right with the half pointer is magnetic north. Note that the declination on this map is 17.5° east. Oregon is on the West Coast and the declination is to the east, just as declination is to the west on the East Coast. Do not let this confuse you.

The best way to determine declination is by simply checking the bottom of a local map. Note that if the map is more than 30 years old, the value may have changed slightly.

GPS receivers automatically make this adjustment and can be programmed to display either true or magnetic north. Remember to convert magnetic north to true north before using compass readings with a map. For example, in the United States:

Declination is Eastern, if West of the Agonic Line, (Western United States). Magnetic bearings are converted to true north by adding the number of declination degrees. "West is Best," reminds you to add.

$60°$ bearing, declination is $13°$ east: $60° + 13° = 73°$ for true north

Declination is Western, if East of the Agonic Line, (Eastern United States). Magnetic bearings are converted to true north by subtracting the number of declination degrees. "East is Least," reminds us to subtract.

$60°$ bearing, declination is $17°$ west: $60° - 17° = 43°$ for true north.

The procedure is reversed to convert true north to magnetic north. Remember the direction does not change, only the bearing number.

Finding North & Orientating the Map

One of the advantages of using a compass is the ability to set or orientate the map to the correction direction when navigating in the field.

1. Rotate the compass azimuth ring or bezel to 0 degrees.
2. Place the compass on the lower section of the map next to the declination scale.
3. Match the lines on the compass body with the north grid lines on the map.
4. Rotate the map with the compass remaining on it until the magnetic needle aligns with the east or west declination degrees shown.

Now you can more efficiently use the map as it is correctly facing the correct direction to align landmarks such as mountains and rivers.

 Compasses are available with mechanically adjustable declination setting 0° to true north. Remember to re-set the declination adjustment if traveling outside your local area.

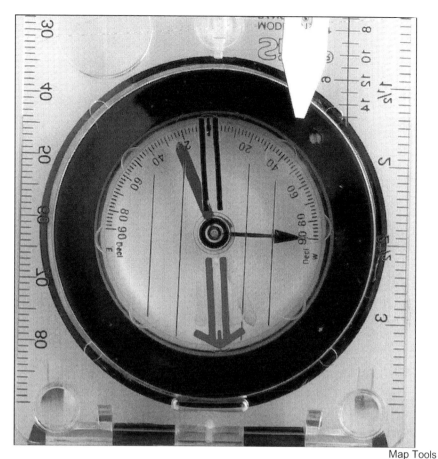

A small screw adjusts the back of the compass to set 0° on the bezel to true north.

Compass Terms

Attack Points One or more landmarks used to reach a nav target.

Back Bearing Reversing a bearing for a return trip. It is 180° in the opposite direction.

Bearing A direction measured by a compass degree needed to travel to stay on a course. Also known as an Azimuth.

Cardinal Points The primary compass points, N, E, S, and W. The Intercardinal Points are NE, SE, SW and NW.

Course The direction between two points, or to reach a navigation target.

Navigation or Target A destination or waypoint to be reached.

Track The actual direction currently being traveled to reach a nav target.

Shooting a bearing with an Orienteering compass. Taking careful aim with this Centerhold Technique reduces error.

Shooting a Compass Bearing

The whole point of packing around a compass is the ability to determine direction and finding a bearing. The compass indicates a direction in magnetic north. From this information, we can determine what bearing degree to travel to reach a navigational target. Compass navigation is based on moving from one landmark to another until the final destination is reached. Here is how it is done:

1. Find an "Attack Point" landmark like a large tree, rock or mountain.

2. Hold the compass close to the body and flat, rotate the body to align with the landmark. Do not hold the compass in front of a metal belt buckle.

3. Rotate the compass bezel ring until the north sided needle is "boxed" by the orienteering arrow. A rhyme to remember is "Put the red in the shed."

4. Check the degree on the bezel ring that aligns with the travel arrow.

5. Take a few readings for accuracy, (shifting your eyes from the compass to the target and back about three times), making final adjustments as the compass is being sighted to the attack point.

6. If using magnetic north, don't forget to adjust the bearing, plus or minus, for declination. Remember the direction does not change, just the bearing.

Try it. It is easier than it sounds and it's fun to practice. From the porch, shoot a bearing to the mailbox. Then to the neighbor's fence. Now back to the garage and back to the porch. In the field, it is wise to write down the bearings traveled to allow the route to be repeated or backtracked. A Back Bearing is reversing a bearing for a return trip. It is 180° in the opposite direction. For example, a bearing of 5° north would require a back or return bearing of 185° south.

 Compasses are magnetized differently for Northern and Southern Hemispheres. Remember to pick up a new compass if your travels take you across the Equator.

Navigation Systems

Degrees or Meters?
The primary two geographic coordinate systems used around the world are Latitude/Longitude and Universal Transverse Mercator, or UTM. Latitude/Longitude, UTM or any other geographic coordinate system can be easily selected in a GPS receiver setup menu. Either system provides a numeric set of coordinates for any location in the world.

Neither one of these navigation systems are difficult to learn. Latitude/longitude is the world's primary system, but the challenge with it is that we don't typically think of distances in terms of Degrees, Minutes and Seconds. UTM is a much easier system but it's based upon metric meters and kilometers, while in the United States, we still measure distance by football fields and miles.

For general navigation it's important to understand the latitude/longitude system. To perform detailed groundwork on topographic maps, it is easier to use the UTM system. Read on and we'll get you on track for both.

Latitude/Longitude
Latitude is a measurement of distance north or south of the Equator. Latitude lines run horizontally around the globe and parallel the earth's equator. The equator separates the globe in Northern and Southern Hemispheres. The equator is 0° with lines stacked horizontally north and south to 90° at each pole. These lines of *Parallel* measure north/south coordinates.

"Latitude /Flatitude" is a way of remembering that these lines run horizontally. They are also referred to as Parallels because they are parallel to the equator.

Longitude is a measurement of distance east or west of the Prime Meridian. Longitude lines circle the globe vertically intersecting the North and South Poles to measure east-west coordinates. The starting point is 0° at Greenwich, England, and wraps around the earth east and west to 180°. The way to remember these lines is by *"Longitude/Longertude."*

These lines are the longest because they do not narrow at the poles like Latitude lines. They are also referred to as *Meridians*, the prime meridian beginning in Greenwich, England. It may make it easier to think of the prime meridian as the vertical version of the Equator on the globe.

Latitude lines are horizontal and measure north/south coordinates.

Longitude lines are vertical and measure east/west coordinates.

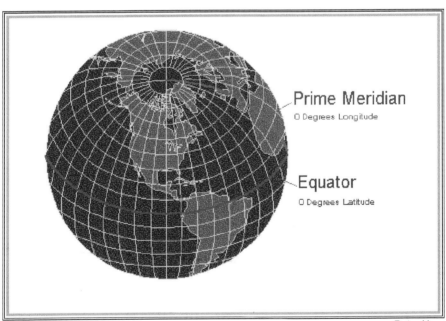

Peter Hana

Globe showing latitude/longitude lines in conjunction with the Prime Meridian and the Equator.

This system uses degrees, minutes and seconds. One degree equals 60 minutes, each minute equals 60 seconds.

1° = 60' (minutes), 1'(minute) = 60" (seconds).

168

That is how Latitude/Longitude coordinates are written, in Degrees°, Minutes' and Seconds."

One Degree = 69.05 statute miles

One Minute = 1 nautical mile or 1.15 statute ground miles

One Second = 100 feet

These distances are for Latitude, but accurate for Longitude only at the equator. This is because the distance between the Longitude lines narrow as they approach the North and South Poles. Due to this factor, the longitude distance decreases as the lines of longitude reach the poles. This is why latitude/longitude grids are rectangle instead of square.

 ***Statute vs. Nautical Mile.* A standard ground mile is known as a *Statute*, with a distance of 5,280 feet. Sailors use the *Nautical* mile. Its length is 6,080 feet which is also the length of a minute.**

Latitude/Longitude Coordinate Address

A confusing issue with the use of this system is that the same address can be displayed in three different formats. The following three address are all for the same longitude coordinate.

1. Full address showing degrees, minutes and seconds. In a GPS receiver this setting looks like: HDDD° MM' SS'S"
   N 43° 41' 58.9"   W 122° 49' 10.7"

2. Decimal minutes which eliminates the seconds. In a GPS receiver this setting looks like: HDDD° MM.MMM'

   N 43° 41.982'   W 122° 49.178'

3. Decimal degrees which eliminates minutes and seconds. In a GPS receiver this setting looks like: HDDD.DDDDD°

   N 43.69970°   W 122.81963°

Latitude is listed first, measuring the north-south position. This address is north of the equator by 43 degrees, 41 minutes and 58.9 seconds.

Longitude is listed second, measuring the east-west position. This address is west of Greenwich, England by 122 degrees, 49 minutes and 10.7 seconds.

Coordinates are listed with a directional letters or positive/negative signs. Latitude numbers north of the Equator are positive numbers. Longitude numbers west of the Prime Meridian are negative numbers.

+ 43° 41' 58.9"   - 122° 49' 10.7"

Universal Transverse Mercator (UTM)

The UTM system uses the metric system of kilometers and meters instead of degrees, minutes, and seconds. Remember the name of this system by the initials of *"**U T**alkin to **M**e?"* UTM coordinates are often considered easier to read, especially if you understand the metric system. Unfortunately, most maps, unless they are detailed topographic, do not include UTM grids or tick marks.

The UTM world grid divides the globe into 60 equal sections called Zones, 6° wide. Each Zone is numbered 1 through 60, beginning at 180° longitude, wrapping around the globe to the east. This system covers between 84° N and 80° S. The area above and below these latitudes, the North and South Poles, are covered by the Universal Polar Stereographic (UPS) grid system. This system is listed in the GPS receiver's Setup menu as UPS/GPS.

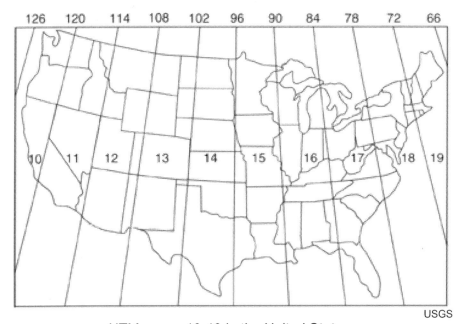

USGS

UTM zones 10-19 in the United States.

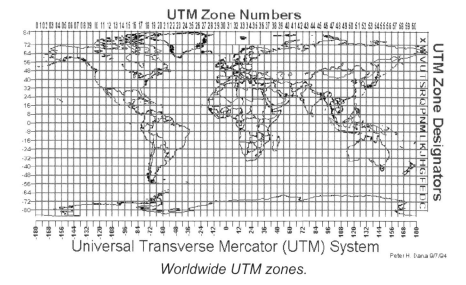

UTM Zone Numbers

Universal Transverse Mercator (UTM) System

Peter H. Dana 9/7/94

Worldwide UTM zones.

Each 6° zone has horizontal and vertical reference lines. A vertical line, known as the Zone Meridian, splits the section into two 3° halves. Vertical and horizontal grid lines are 1,000 meters or one kilometer apart. Coordinates indicate the number of meters east from the beginning zone line, *Easting*, and how many meters north or south from the Equator, *Northing*. This is how the coordinates are always read, to the right, Easting, then up, Northing.

Easting is the horizontal east/west measurement that indicates the number of kilometers and meters the coordinate is east from the start of the zone line. The numbers increase moving left to right, west to east. Each zone's meridian begins with 500,000.

Northing is the vertical north/south measurement that indicates the number of kilometers and meters the coordinate is north or south of the Equator. The number at the equator in the Northern Hemisphere is 00**00**000. This number increases moving north. In the Southern Hemisphere, the number at the equator begins with 100**00**000, and decreases moving south.

Here is a set of UTM coordinates:

10 T   06**24**301 E,   48**59**317 N

This is how UTM coordinates are broken down:

(**10**) indicates the coordinates are in the 10th world zone. Note on the above UTM maps, this vertical zone is in the Western United States.

171

(**T**) indicates the world zone designator. This horizontal zone covers the Northern United States.

(**0624301**) is the Easting as indicated by the (E) at the end of the number. Each zone's meridian begins with 500,000, therefore this location is 124,301 meters, or 124.3 kilometers east of the zone's meridian.

(**4859317**) is the Northing as indicated by the (N) at the end of the number. Knowing that the number at the equator in the Northern Hemisphere is 00**00**000. This location is 4,859,317 meters or 4,859.3 kilometers north of the Equator.

The larger two numbers are called the *Principal Digit*. These correspond with the coordinates that run along the top, bottom and sides of the map. The principal digit numbers are one kilometer, or 1,000 meters apart. This is what makes UTM coordinates easier to read, knowing that map grid lines are in 1,000-meter blocks.

This system is often considered easier to use for the following reasons:

- No negative or decimal point coordinates.
- The grids are square allowing coordinates to be more easily measured.
- Coordinates translate directly into a more recognizable measurement format of kilometers and meters.
- Points on a map can be selected by site with accuracy within 50 meters.

 The UTM kilometer grid system is easy to read once you are familiar with the metric system. Remember a meter is just longer than a yard (39.37 inches), and 1,000 meters (a kilometer), equals .62 of a mile.

Selecting a Coordinate System

The system you decide to use should be based upon the type of navigating you are doing. Here are some issues to consider:

If you are working within a group, a primary factor should be to use whatever system the group is using.

The latitude/longitude system is preferred by long range travelers such as pilots and sailors.

The UTM system is best for detailed groundwork, such as in exploring and mining. The system is typically limited to detailed topographic maps from 1:24,000 to 1:250,000.

Often the maps available will dictate what system you use. United States Geological Survey, USGS topographic maps include UTM grids. Other less detailed maps only include latitude/longitude grids.

Township, Range & Section

The Federal Township, Range and Section (TRS), grids are used in the United States primarily west of the state of Ohio. This system was developed by the U.S. Government as early as 1784 as a more accurate and standardized system to survey land. You will not find this system in a GPS receiver, but it is good to understand how it works. Mining claims are marked this way and it is not uncommon to find TRS markers in the field that can confirm a location on topo map.

This system divides land into 36 approximately square mile units called Townships. Each Township has a Township and Range designation to define its 36 square mile area. The horizontal rows are the Township designation. Township coordinates are numbered and listed as north or south from a selected latitude baseline. The vertical rows are the Range designation. Range coordinates are numbered and listed as west or east of a selected principle meridian of longitude.

Townships are divided into 36, one square mile, 640-acre parcels called Sections. The Sections are numbered from 1 to 36 within the Township. Section one begins in the northeast corner as the numbers proceed west, then east, alternately down each row, ending with 36 in the southeast corner.

6					1
7					12
18					13
19					24
30					25
31					36

Sections are divided into quarters, which are further quartered to describe a property location. For example, the legal description for the Utah Geological Survey's former office on Foothill Drive is written: SE ¼, NW ¼, Section 23, T.1 S., R.1 E., of the Salt Lake Base Line.

This system is good for finding a general direction but lacks serious accuracy without further description. A quarter of the Section is 166 acres. To get within 40 acres, a Section requires being divided two more times, such as the NW ¼ of the SW ¼.

Metal yellow section markers or location posters can be found in the field that specify TRS coordinates. The Township and Range coordinates of this 36 square mile Township are indicated on the top. Wilderness roads are often numbered to correspond to this system. For example, a road numbered *10N59* may indicate that it began in Township 10 North.

The TRS system can appear outdated and confusing, although it is important to know because it is still so commonly used in plotting real property. Most topographic and U.S. Forest Service maps include the grid and coordinates that appear in red. Range numbers are on the top and bottom of a map, and Township numbers are on the left and right sides.

The Least You Need to Know

- Basic navigation can be determined from nature, such as the location of the sun and stars.

- A compass and paper maps are still needed, even if using GPS.

- Accurate navigation requires the understanding of Declination.

- Learning to shoot and follow a compass bearing is the basis of all navigation.

- Know the advantages to using both the Latitude/Longitude and UTM coordinate systems.

- Learning the Township, Range and Section system can be useful for mining claims and confirming your location on a map.

13. MAP READING

Paper or Digital, Map Reading is Critical, Even With GPS

Map reading is the cornerstone of navigation. Whether using GPS or not, your ability to get around in unknown territory will depend on how well you can read a map. Maps come in all shapes and sizes, both paper and electronic. Yes, GPS receivers include a base map, but they will not completely replace paper. Map reading skills are consistent regardless of the form of map you use.

Though road maps can get you to the trail head, we are going to focus on mapping you would use for off-road travel and exploration which is going to be small scale, detailed topo maps.

 Maps are referred to as *small* or *large* scale. Small scale maps cover a limited area in great detail, from 1:24,000 to 1:65,500. Large scale maps are like state or highway maps that show a larger area in less detail.

When viewing a map, check out the specs along the bottom before trying to find your position in the middle. This collar area is full of reference information that will provide aid in its reading. This information includes the scale, the legend, distance indicators, color codes, magnetic declination, map datum and the year the map was published. The gridlines and tick marks around the edges determine what coordinates are provided. Reviewing this information will help ensure the selection of a map in the scale and detail appropriate for your application.

Topographic Maps

The most detailed maps are topos that are 1:24 in scale. They are called 7.5-minute maps because they cover 7.5 minutes of latitude and longitude. That's an area approximately 6.5 miles wide, 8.5 miles long, and 55 square miles. In this highly detailed scale where one-inch on the map equals 2,000 feet on the ground. In the United States, these maps are created by the U.S Geological Survey (USGS).

Another advantage of topographic maps is that they provide a three-dimensional prospective of the ground. This is done using contour lines that indicate terrain structure and elevation. Topographic maps also include the primary geographic coordinate systems of latitude/longitude, UTM and Township, Range and Section.

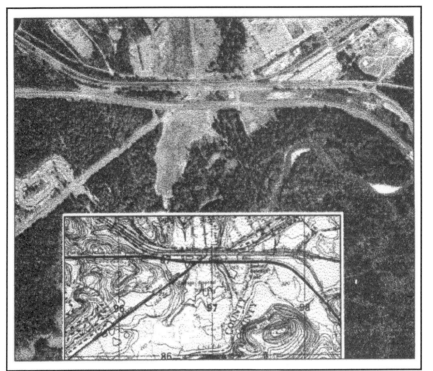

Detailed topo maps are created from aerial and satellite imagery.

Map Features

Map reading skills are universal, regardless of the map's scale or type. Map reading is essentially the interpretation of lines, features, landmarks and symbols on a map. It helps to think about the map in a three-dimensional way, instead of just a flat sheet of paper. This is done by focusing on major landmarks and high and low elevation features. Contour lines on topographic maps make this easier as the lines profile the terrain.

It is helpful to maintain the 'big picture' of the area in which you are traveling by keeping major landmarks in perspective. Prominent features, being man-made or natural, include all major landmarks such as mountains, highways, waterways, and bridges.

Prominent features are good to use as a reference in conjunction with a map in order to determine your general location. Baseline features are linear reference points such as roads, rivers, and power lines. These natural boundaries are ideal to follow or use as a return point.

In the field, maps are easier to read if they are set to the terrain, matching the prominent and baseline features on the map with those on the ground. This is known as *Terrain Association*.

This orientation helps reference landmarks and gives the user a better understanding of what lies ahead. This is done with the assistance of a compass by rotating the map until the top faces true north.

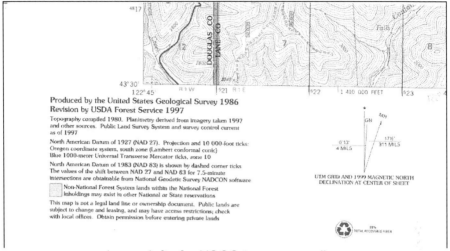

Lower left of a USGS topo map collar.

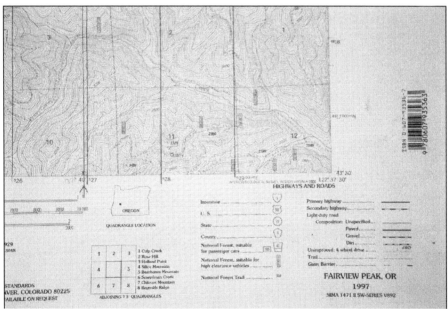

Lower right of a USGS topo map collar.

Reading Topographic Maps

Our example is a 7.5-minute topo map of the *Bohemia Mining District*, south of Cottage Grove, Oregon. This map was located by reviewing a State of Oregon USGS map coverage index to find the map of our exact area of interest.

The state index map is divided into titled 7.5-minute sections. Our map is titled *Fairview Peak Quadrangle-Oregon*. The bottom section of the map gives details that include the following:

Date Produced in 1986, revised in 1997. Topographic information is from 1980.

Datum North American Datum of 1927 (NAD 27). The datum is the global survey system used to create the map. This is important because GPS receivers need to be programmed to the same datum used to create the map.

Declination Diagram The scale indicating the degree a compass is adjusted to correct Magnetic North to True North. This map's declination is 17.5 degrees as of 1999.

Map Scale 1:24,000, one-inch equals 24,000 inches on the ground.

Mileage scale One mile equals about 2-5/8 inches.

Contour Interval The elevation lines are 40' apart, every 5th darker brown line indicates the elevation in feet.

Misc. Information Where this map is located in relation to the state, map names surrounding this map and list of symbols for highways and roads.

 Contour lines are the curvy brown lines on a topographic map that indicate the shape of the terrain. Every fifth darker brown line is the Elevation Index line. This line indicates the elevation in feet or meters.

Check the Datum

When using GPS with any map, be sure to program the GPS to the correct datum used in creating the map. Many United States topo maps use North American Datum 1927 [NAD 27 CONUS], or possibly the datum used in Geocaching, World Geodetic System 1984 [WGS 84].

In Europe, it is the Ordnance Survey Great Britain [OSGB]. The receiver is set to default to a datum. Check the Setup menu to ensure it is the correct datum for your application. Failing to make this adjustment can cause errors in calculations as much as 1,000 meters.

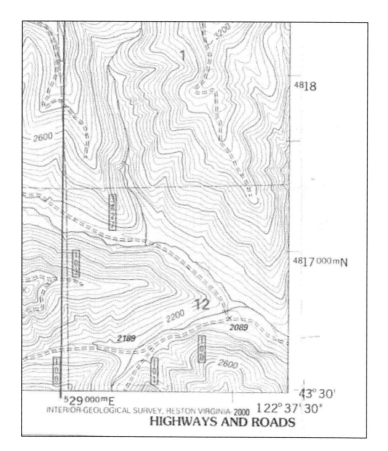

Grid Lock

Notice from the corner of this topographic map, that there are tick-marks, lines and numbers everywhere. Besides latitude/longitude and UTM coordinates, there are red grids that are for township, range and section. When referencing numbers and tick marks, be sure you are referencing the correct markings before taking any readings.

The above map includes all of the following coordinates:

4818   UTM Northing

4817000mN   Full UTM Northing

529000mE   Full UTM Easting (lower left)

43° 30' 43   Degrees Latitude

122° 37' 30"   Degrees Longitude (lower right)

1 & 12   are (TRS) sections

A map ruler will allow the transfer of coordinates from a map to be entered as a waypoint in a GPS receiver just as waypoint coordinates can be plotted on a map.

Map Colors and Symbols

Topographic maps are color-coded and covered with symbols and markings. Fortunately, most are relatively self-explanatory. For example, using on the color codes, black is used to designate roads, buildings, and other man-made objects. Blue is used to designate waterways and brown is used for the contour lines.

Contour Lines

Contour lines show the map's topography by indicating the shape of the terrain and its elevation. These lines make it possible to determine the height of the terrain or the depths of bodies of water. These lines do not cross each other because they join points of equal elevation. Every fifth line is darker and is known as an *Index Line*. The Index lines provide the specific elevation listed in feet or meters above sea level. On our example topo, the elevation is listed in feet. There is a distance of 40 feet between each line, equaling 200 feet between each index line. The amount of distance between each line is known as the *Contour Interval*.

Contour lines provide a low-tech way for a map to come alive by providing a three-dimensional view of the terrain. Reading these lines is simple, the closer the lines are together, the steeper the terrain. Open spaced contoured areas are flat, heavily lined areas are steep or cliff walls. With "V" shaped contours, the tip of the v points uphill, as seen with creeks and rivers. "U" shaped contours typically point downhill. The following are typical terrain features found:

A. "V" shaped lines point to upriver. In this example, a creek is flowing down into a larger river.

B. Mountain Peak represented by circular contour lines becoming smaller to the top.

C. Spurs most likely caused by an ancient creek.

D. Saddle where a plateau joins two mountain peaks.

E. Cliff wall as indicated by a concentration of contour lines.

F. "U" shaped lines point downhill.

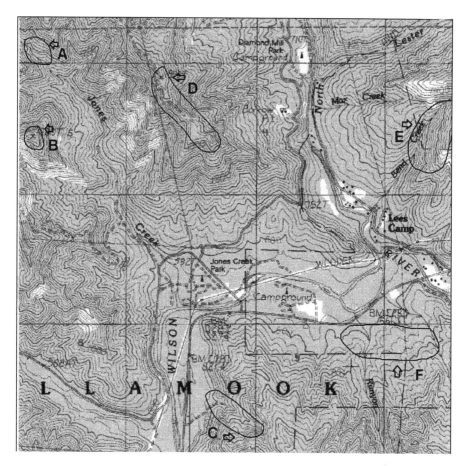

Maps can be inaccurate and outdated. Not surprisingly, locations on the ground often look entirely different than what you might think they would look like from a map.

Navigation Tips and Tricks

Combining the traditional map and compass skills with a few tips will have you navigating like a pro in no time. Understanding these skills also enables you to use your GPS receiver to the fullest potential. Here's a list of useful navigation skills to help keep you on track:

Aiming Off This is traveling on a compass bearing in an indirect path to your target. This is done to bypass an obstacle, or to help find a target on a linear feature. For example, you believe your truck is parked on a roadway straight ahead at about 5°. You cannot see the vehicle due to dense vegetation, so you aim off slightly to the right at 15° knowing that when you reach the roadway, the car will be to our left.

Calculate Map Distances Keep a small piece of wire in your navigation kit for measuring distances on a map. Bend the wire to follow a road or trail and then straighten it out to find the distance using the map scale.

Catch features These are features that indicate that you have missed a turn or have traveled too far. If circumstances make a destination difficult to find, know what roads or features are beyond the location. That way you will know if you have traveled too far if you reach the catch feature you have chosen.

Confirm Location by Elevation Altimeters are a useful way to help confirm your location on a map. Compare altimeter elevation readings with map markings. Remember a GPS receiver's altimeter may not be as accurate as a manual barometric altimeter.

Dead Reckoning Is used to confirm your location by recording your travels from a last known position. It requires keeping track of every distance and bearing traveled. Starting from a known position, record your route on a map or in a journal. This is an ideal way to back up a GPS receiver when traveling in unknown territory.

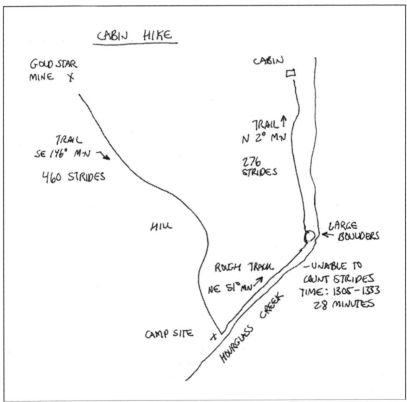

Notes kept from compass bearing and pacing while Dead Reckoning.

Directions from Nature Remember the basics - the sun rises in the east, moves to the south, then sets in the west. At night, find the North Star. Also, the points on a crest moon point south.

Night Navigation When traveling in darkness, remember our natural night vision takes about 30 minutes to fully develop. Red LED lights or flashlight filters work great for producing adequate light without losing night vision. Besides using GPS, keep track of time and use pacing to maintain your position. Remember pacing steps will be considerably shorter at night and be sure that your compass glows in the dark.

Pacing Pacing is a way to measure distance while walking by knowing the length of your stride (both right and left footsteps). For example, as a 6' tall man, my stride is 60" or five feet. This can be helpful for measuring distance from point to point while on foot.

Reverse Perspective While traveling, remember to turn around and look for the reverse perspective. This is what the road or trail will look like when you return. Every few minutes, take a 360° scan. Notice the scenery and landmarks in every direction, paying special attention to what it looks like behind you.

Trail Markers Manually back up your track log the old-fashion way by blazing a trail with markers. Use natural resources like bent twigs or placing rocks. Draw arrows in the dirt with a stick or cut marks in tree bark. Homemade marking kits work great and are easy to make using thumbtacks and colored survey ribbon. Do not forget to remove the markers on the return leg.

Triangulation We learned how to use triangulation to confirm the location of a cache. In this application, your location can be confirmed by shooting a bearing to at least two or more different surrounding landmarks. A current location is determined by plotting the intersection of the bearings on a map.

 Use your compass to orientate your map to ensure it is facing the correct direction. This will allow you to compare and match map features to what you are seeing on the ground.

 One of the most useful navigation tricks is taking a reverse prospective. Turn around frequently and see what the trail looks like behind you. This will be your view for your return trip.

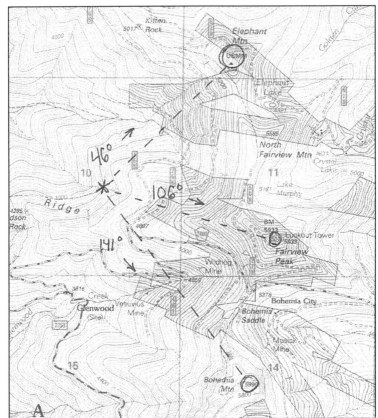

Example of Triangulation by shooting a compass bearing at three different mountain peaks to plot oneself on a map.

The Least You Need to Know

- Small scale topo maps are used for off-road travel and exploration.

- Map reading is easier after reviewing the map's details located on the collar.

- Remember to set your GPS to the same Datum as your map.

- Learning to read contour lines brings topo maps to life with a 3-D effect.

- Learn a number of navigation tips will have you trailblazing like a pro.

14. USING GPS NAVIGATION

DoD's gift to Overlanders!

The U.S. Military spent billions of dollars to create an accurate worldwide navigation system and we get to use it for free. Well, free after we spend hundreds of dollars on a good receiver. But it is worth it. No other form of technology has made travel easier and safer on or off the road than GPS.

GPS, an acronym for Global Positioning System, is a gift from the U.S. Department of Defense. Twenty-four satellites with a couple of spares, broadcast special radio signals down to earth that are intercepted by GPS receivers. Each receivers' computer analyzes the signals to determine its location anywhere in the world through triangulation. Now you can save your favorite locations through a *Waypoint*, and leave an electronic bread crumb trail, a *Tracklog*. These two features alone make getting lost, almost impossible.

GPS receivers are called receivers because once they lock onto four or more of the 12 satellites in each hemisphere, you now have accuracy around 30 feet or nine meters. The U.S. Government, as well as other governments, broadcast additional ground-based radio signals to supplement satellite signals making GPS even more accurate. The U.S Government GPS site indicates 6.2 feet (1.8 meters) 95% of the time. That is certainly close enough for you to find your hidden mining claim, *Geocache* or camp site.

Using GPS

There are many handheld GPS receiver options available that are used by everyone in the outdoors from hikers to hunters. I have a handheld in my bugout bag although they have small screens difficult to read for off-road driving and rely on disposable batteries. Vehicle-based GPS receivers will always be the go-to for off-road navigation, being hard-wired, bigger screens and reliable. Screens can be 5" to 12" that are powered by the vehicle's electrical system.

The limitations are few and benefits are many. You just need to make sure there is a working power cable to the unit and the GPS antenna has a clear view of the sky. GPS satellite radio signals operate on line-of-site. They will travel through a car windshield, but not through a metal roof. You may also have some interference from cliff walls and tall city buildings. When in doubt, get out in the open so you can get four or more satellites locked in for improved accuracy. The GPS receiver will have a page that indicates satellite reception and estimated accuracy.

Even if your sense of direction is great and you don't mind getting lost on occasion, there are other important reasons to install a GPS on the dash. The first is accurate speed. Larger tires show a slower speedometer, but GPS speed is accurate. Many street receivers also show what the current speed limit is, and the number turns red when you go over. This is extremely helpful on road trips where the speed limit is not adequately posted. Knowing this information makes it easier to accurately set your cruise control.

Another huge advantage is knowing your altitude. Altitude provides a useful reference to your location. Driving through mountains you can also see snow and ice levels based upon altitude levels. There is usually an option to an on-screen volt indicator providing a way to monitor your battery level. Two Trip Calculators are also helpful as one can be used for oil changes and the second to track your current adventure.

Regardless of the brand, size or price, GPS receivers are designed to provide the same basic functions. More expensive models provide a greater memory storage capability. They also provide an improved base map display. The following are useful features they provide:

Alarms An alarm notifies the user of an approaching waypoint.

Altimeter Elevation data accurate to 25 feet.

Antenna Built in or an antenna jack.

Base Map Basic digital map image to detailed topo and satellite images.

Computer Interface USB Data in/out capability allows the unit to receive, (upload) data from a computer, or send, (download) data to a computer. Data includes; Maps, Waypoints, Tracklogs and Routes.

Course Up vs. North Up Most use *Course Up* so your icon is always moving up on the screen.

Display Screen With your current position as a pointer indicating direction of travel.

Electronic Compass Will work best when driving over 4 MPH.

Go To Feature Select a waypoint, address or point of interest and most receivers will provide auto routing turn-by-turn directions. Miss a turn and the until will recalculate the route. Basic chart plotter styles (for off-road use), give you an arrow to target with the distance.

Memory Data Port SD card slot for additional map or satellite image detail provide by GPS or aftermarket suppliers.

Routes A series of waypoints listed in sequence from start to finish to reach a final destination. Then route can be reversed for the trip back home.

Search Feature To find waypoints, addresses or points of interest.

Track Log Plots an electronic breadcrumb trail as a sequence of dots or track points, showing a path traveled.

Time of Day, Date Based upon accurate satellite data.

Waypoints The ability to save and store locations. Then select saved waypoints or any other location in the unit's database for directions for traveling to that location.

Waypoint Averaging Allows greater accuracy in saving waypoints by recording the position over an amount of time.

Setting Up Your Receiver

Get the receiver hard-mounted in your truck with a fused hard-wired power supply. Next, see if your built-in antenna works well or, better yet, if you need to place a remote antenna on the roof. Once everything is good to go, turn on the power button and wait for satellites to get locked on. You should see a message that states, "Looking for satellites," until it changes to "Ready to Navigate."

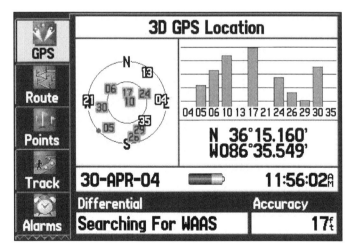

Garmin

Depending on the brand and model you may have a satellite reception screen that provides the number of satellites locked and accuracy.

187

Review the owner's manual to see what features your receiver has to offer. You might be surprised with the all the options available. You also need to make some choices on how you will set up the receiver. Here are some considerations:

 When working within a group, agree in advance on the following, then set your GPS to correct values: 1. Map coordinates, Lat/Long or UTM? If Lat/Long, full address or decimal point? 2. Which north, True or Magnetic? 3. Which Map Datum?

Coordinates Choose if you want your receiver to display Latitude/Longitude or UTM. If you choose Lat/Long, there are two popular choices; Degrees, Minutes and Seconds [HDDD° MM' SS.S"], or degrees with decimal minutes [HDDD° MM.MMM"]. The UTM selection looks like [UPS/UTM].

Distance Measurement Distance and speed can be measured in statute or nautical miles, or metric kilometers. Based upon your selection, altitude will be displayed in either feet or meters.

Map Datum The receiver may default to WGS 84. In North America, other common datums include NAD27 CONUS and NAD83.

Map Page Orientation This sets the direction of the Map Page to north up or direction of travel up.

North True North or Magnetic North.

There should also be options to what data can be displayed on the home page screen. This includes the following:

- Compass Bearing or Cardinal Point
- Current Coordinates
- Elevation
- Distance to Next Waypoint
- Estimated Time of Arrival to Next Waypoint
- Speed in MPH or KPH
- Time of Day, 12 or 24 hour format

The best way to familiarize yourself with new gear is to simply turn it on, get a satellite fix and check the features. Scroll through the pages and customize the receiver to make it provide the information you need.

Most GPS receivers provide a Trip Computer feature. Set the computer before your next trek to check out interesting data. These include: Trip Odometer, Average Speed, Trip Timer and Maximum Speed.

Types of Vehicle-Based Receivers

I like vehicle-based GPS receivers because they are hard-wired and reliable with no cell coverage or Wi-Fi needed. They are also practical and easy to use. The center icon shows your location and direction of travel with a constant tracklog. Marking a waypoint requires just a push of a button. They are also durable. Once securely mounted and wired in, they should withstand years of vibration, dust and extreme temperatures.

Vehicle based receivers are going to fall into three primary categories: OEM factory units, street navigation or marine chart plotter style.

OEM Factory GPS

Auto manufacturers have been integrating factory GPS receivers with their vehicles' entertainment systems for years. The advantage to these units is they are built in, in the center of the dash and ready to go. The disadvantages are that they are difficult or expensive to update. The auto dealer will want to sell you proprietary disks used to update the system that are most likely outdated before they are ever installed.

These factory systems maybe also be cumbersome to use, like Jeep's system will not allow the search programing functions to be used while the vehicle is in motion. These factory units will probably not provide critical features like saving waypoints or tracklogs. The bottom line is they can be handy because there are already there, front and center, but will most likely never be as accurately updated as aftermarket units that can be easily plugged into a computer and updated.

Street Navigation GPS

Street units provide a behind the vehicle view showing just a small section of road in front of you, providing typically accurate search features for address and other points of interest with turn-by-turn directions. These receivers typically provide a driver point-of-view where you are looking at the rear of your vehicle icon on a map at about a 45° angle.

This view works best for street driving as it shows you just enough of the horizon to get the next turn in the route.

It doesn't give you the big picture however that a flatter map would give you. *Garmin* pretty much rules this market followed by *Tom Tom* and *Magellan*.

Factory GPS can be useable if you can keep them updated. This Jeep Wrangler has GPS mapping from Garmin which is great. The problem is you must stop to program or search.

Street navigation uses a 45° angle driver's view that works best for turn-by-turn directions.

Marine Chart Plotter GPS

Serious off-roaders have gone to the marine chart plotter style receivers. These provide a flat bird's eye view of where you have been and where you are going, that is more useful for overland. These 'fish finder' marine chart plotters can have poor or no search features and no turn-by-turn directions, but they are the standard for off-road racing and driving.

They offer a flat overhead view that provides a better reference of the landscape, showing you where you been and where you are going. They use SD memory card slots to enhance the factory map or load waypoint and tracklog information for expedition travel and racing. *Lowrance* primarily rules this market as the standard of what most off-roaders are using from Baja to Moab.

John Lucasey, Gaasit.com

Most off-roaders, pre-runners and racers use a flat, birds eye view offered by marine style chart plotters by Lowrance.

The *Magellan TRX7* and the *Garmin Overlander* are unique in that they are designed for off-road use, but also provide street level searches and turn-by-turn directions. They both provide preloaded topo maps, trails, campgrounds as well as user-based supported websites. For *Magellan*, www.trxtrailhead.com and for *Garmin*, www.ioverlander.com. These sites are very useful by providing crowd-sourced trail ratings with detailed feedback by its users.

191

This includes additional points of interest, photos, and waypoints. Even information on conditions of rock, mud, water and snow, what ground clearance is needed as well as if high or low range 4WD is required. All very useful to help determine if your rig is up to the task to challenge the route.

Magellan TRX7

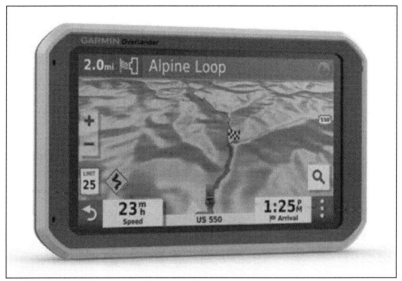

Garmin Overlander

We have high hopes for these crossover receiver units that bridge the gap between off-road crowd-sourced data and street level turn-by-turn direction GPS units.

Navigation in the Field

Let us get down to the business of navigating. When it comes to GPS, there are three things you need to learn: saving *Waypoints*, using *Track logs* and creating *Routes*.

 Holding down the GOTO or MOB button on most receivers saves the current location as a *Man Overboard* waypoint. This feature is designed as a one-button method for immediately marking and navigating back to a location.

Saving Waypoints

One of the primary functions of using GPS, is saving and traveling to waypoints. A waypoint is a selected location of interest that is stored in the receiver's memory. This allows you to return to the same location as well as share this information with someone else.

Once the receiver is up and running, the first waypoint to save is in your own driveway. Your receiver may have an option for a Home waypoint and return button, or you just might have to select the current location and title it, 'HOME.' This is helpful because regardless of wherever you are at in the world, the Home waypoint can be recalled determining how far in distance and time to return.

Garmin provides a Home waypoint feature and is an option on the Go To page as seen in the lower left part of the screen.

Saving waypoints is important because it gives you a perspective of your travel area. Save lots, they are free. If you don't need it, delete it, but you never know when you might want to return. You won't remember what 004 means next month, so give each waypoint a name to give it meaning. Like *Trial Head, Camp Site, Test Mine 1*, etc. There are several ways to save waypoints. Here is a list of seven:

Marking Current Position This is one the most common and easiest methods. Holding down the Enter/Mark button or touch the vehicle icon on the home screen and a message should appear asking you to save the current position. Once you do, the name will default to the next number in line. Go that field and change the number to a name that will allow you to remember it.

Entering Manually Enter the numeral coordinates manually using the Rocker Keypad or touchscreen. Note that you will have to change the coordinate system you are using if the ones you are entering manually are different than what you are displaying. For example, if you are using Latitude/Longitude, and the coordinates you want to enter are UTM, change your system over to UTM to accept them. You can always change it back when you are done. The new coordinates will be displayed in the system you choose.

Selecting From Base Map Using the rocker keypad or touchscreen, select a location on your home screen that you would like to save. With a rocker keypad, hit enter or touch the screen with a touchscreen until you get a message asking if you want to save the location.

From a Computer Geocaching style number two, previously saved waypoints and routes are loaded from a computer to the receiver. This is done through selecting a computer interface data transfer option within the receiver and the use of a data cable.

Name Search If a city, point of interest or business is in your receiver's database, you can search by name, find and save it.

Marking a MOB Position Marine style chart plotters have a *Man Overboard* button that is for exactly what it sounds like. A one button push immediately saves a waypoint.

Entering a Projected Position Some receivers may give you the option to enter a compass bearing and distance information to project and save a new waypoint.

Once waypoints are saved, the data can be modified at any time. The name, symbol and coordinates can be manually changed or deleted.

Waypoint Averaging

If the location is critical, your receiver will most likely provide the option of *Waypoint Averaging*. The receiver saves the location then allows more time for the overhead satellites to continue to improve the accuracy. For example, a standard waypoint might be within 16 feet. After a couple minutes of averaging, the accuracy is down to 3 feet.

Navigating to Waypoints

Want to return to your hidden slice of paradise or you think you might be getting turned around on the trail? No problem, just select the nearest or most relevant waypoint and '*Go To*' that location. The receiver will calculate a route to the waypoint selected. Depending on what type of receiver you have, you will get turn-by-turn directions or if using a chart plotter style, a direction arrow and a countdown distance to the location.

Be aware that off-road your receiver maybe giving you directions on roads that do not exist or directions that are based upon line-of-site. It's up to you to find and drive on paths to get you where you want to go. That is the advantage of using a *Tracklog* which we will cover next. As you travel, an electronic breadcrumb trail is being created and appears on your home screen to backtrack on. It is that simple, not getting lost has never been so much fun.

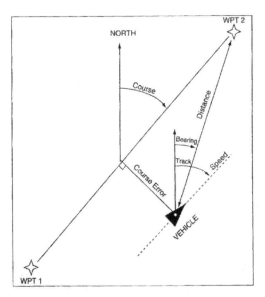

GPS terminology by Garmin International. The bottom line is to go where the GPS tells you to and you are good about 95% of the time.

*Going through my saved waypoints I find the first one
for the initial turn off for the Ponderosa Mine.*

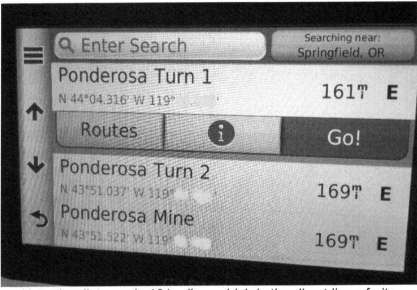

*Note the distance is 161 miles, which is the direct line-of-site.
Once the waypoint is selected the distance increases to
accommodate the roads need to get there.*

Sometimes the receiver will ask you to navigate in a line-of-site to the target. Unless you are flying or sailing, that is almost impossible. It is up to you to drive smart and find a way to get around obstacles to reach your waypoint.

Track Logs

A track log is an electronic breadcrumb trail that is stored and displayed by the receiver. This log indicates the path you have traveled, greatly reducing the chance of becoming lost. Following a previously stored electronic track allows you to literally retrace your steps to backtrack to a previous position.

This feature requires two elements to work properly. First, there must be a continual satellite fix during the duration of the track. If coverage is broken, blanks will appear in the track. The second element is adequate memory available to record the track.

Most receivers are somewhat limited in storage capacity. Depending on the unit's setting, one of two things will happen if the track log memory becomes full. The receiver will stop recording or it will automatically delete older track data. Most receivers provide the option of programming the track log as follows:

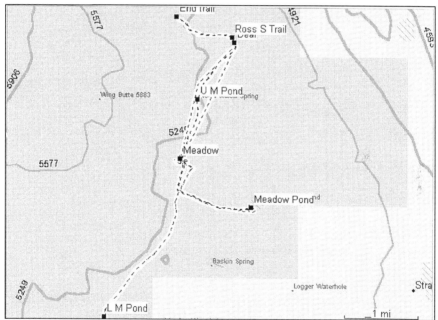

A saved track log with waypoints from a
Central Oregon off-road adventure.

Fill This option records track log data until the memory is full. A text warning message may appear when the memory is full. This option is useful when returning to a starting position is most important.

197

Wrap Under this option, data is continually recorded. This is done by recording over the earliest saved data. This is useful when the latest saved data is most important.

Some receivers may allow you to adjust the number of tracks recorded, this is known as *Interval Value*. For example, the number of tracks dropped are reduced by half if you want to drive from Anchorage Alaska to Cabo San Lucas, Mexico and have the entire trip on the same tracklog.

Saving Track Logs

Track logs are saved just as waypoints and routes. First, clear any previously saved unnecessary track log data if your receiver will allow you to do so. If necessary, adjust the interval value to increase or decrease the track points based upon your application.

After the trip, select to record the track log. Most receivers will then save the track log in a reduced number of track points and title the log with the current date. Like waypoints, rename the track log.
If you need lots of track log detail, you can always record and save multiple track logs, like possibly for *Baja North* and *Baja South*.

Remember the following when saving a track log:

- Clear the track log at the starting point of the new trip.

- Save the track log at the completion of the trip and add name.

- Be sure that the receiver is operational during the entire time of the trip. Lost satellite signals or power will result in a discontinuous log.

Routes

A route is a series of waypoints that are listed in the order of start to finish. Routes may contain up to 30-100 waypoints depending on the capacity of the receiver. Each section between two waypoints is a *Leg*. To create a route, select a series of waypoints in the sequence as they are to be followed.

Routes are beneficial because, unless flying or sailing, it is difficult to travel in a straight line. Obstacles require us to travel indirect paths until the destination is reached. This feature provides direction by organizing waypoints in the flow of travel.

Following a route not only makes navigation easier, it also reduces the risk of error.

Multiple waypoints may not mean much by themselves but, when saved in a route, they are given order, making an easy sequence to follow. Routes also provide us with a planned backtrack when it's time return.

 For street-based auto routing GPS receivers, be sure to update the maps every six months from the manufacturer. Auto routing will lead you astray with outdated maps.

Auto Routing for Street Receivers

Street navigation receivers use *Auto Routing* to do this automatically. When a waypoint is selected, the computer calculates a series of points based upon each turn it takes to get to the final destination waypoint. This system works amazingly well if your receiver includes a business and address database of the location you are looking for.

For example, using the search field, just enter the name of the campground in Moab, Utah, and a few seconds later you have an ETA of the miles and hours it takes to drive there. The user does not realize the points in the route until the receiver tells them to take the next turn. A receiver with the auto routing feature can typically be programed to create routes in various ways and will also consider the type and size of vehicle such as a motorhome vs a car.

Auto routing programmability could include reaching the location by the fastest time, shortest distance, or a direct line in an *off-road* mode. Radio wave data can provide additional real-time information on traffic conditions and weather and re-direct you accordingly to make your trip even smoother. The trick is to update your base map data on a regular basis from an online computer connection to acquire the most recent information available to auto route from.

This system is ideal for streets with names and addresses, but not so much for off-road because you usually cannot travel in a direct path and there are no street or address data to auto route from.

Saving Routes

From chart plotter or hand-held receiver, routes are created from saved waypoints in an order you choose, or from track logs. The following are six examples on how to save routes:

Entered While Traveling Save waypoints along the way, then add them into a new route.

Manually Selected Previously saved waypoints are manually selected from the receiver's database to create a new route.

From a Map Plan your trip by selecting coordinates off a map, converting them into waypoints and adding them into a route. This can be done directly into the receiver or into mapping software to be uploaded into a receiver.

Loaded from a Computer Previously recorded routes can be loaded into a receiver using mapping software and a data cable or transferred from one receiver to another using SD cards.

From a Saved Track Log Using the map Pointer Arrow, select key locations to save as waypoints along a track log.

Use *TracBack* Feature This is a *Garmin* feature, but other manufactures may have something similar. Activating this option creates a 30-waypoint route from the most previously saved track log.

Now that you know how to use your GPS, it's almost impossible to get lost. Find your street with no name and throttle down!

Once a route is saved, data is displayed on an *Active Route Page*. It includes the distance between each waypoint and the total distance of the route. Detailed information is available for each leg of the trip including the distance between waypoints, compass bearing and ETA. Routes can also be easily edited by adding or deleting waypoints.

When a route is saved, the default name will be the date it was created. The route can be renamed at any time. An advantage to using routes is that they are reversible. Once the last waypoint destination is reached, the route is reversed by an Invert command to backtrack to the starting point.

Best in the Desert racing association provided 16 start to finish waypoints for their over 500-mile 'Vegas to Reno' desert race.

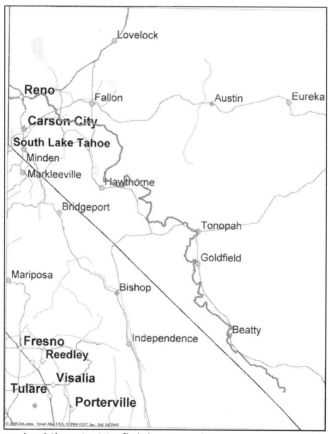

Once we had the start to finish waypoints, we pre-ran the course creating an exact track log for the race. We then added additional waypoints for pit stops, fueling and 'major danger' locations.

Another advantage is that route data can be shared for someone else to follow. For example, the desert race pre-runner runs the course first to save track log, waypoint, and route data. This file can then be transferred to other GPS receivers and computers using a cable or SD card. This allows the race team to load the data to be used in the race car and chase or support vehicles.

A trick used to keep the primary track log clean, is to create a *Trash Track* for unwanted travel areas like diving to the course that can be deleted. Then once ready to travel the desired area, start and title the new track log.

The Least You Need to Know

- GPS is the greatest advancement in overland travel since the invention of 4WD.

- Using GPS is so useful, it's worth taking the time learn the many features available.

- Street receivers with the over the vehicle map view and auto routing are ideal for on-road navigation.

- Marine style chart plotters with a flat map view provide a greater land prospective for off-road navigation.

- The more useful thing you can do with GPS is learning to save and go to waypoints.

- Track logs leave an electronic breadcrumb trail that makes it almost impossible to get lost.

- Routes are useful for trip planning by mapping out every leg of your journey, then reversing the path to return.

15. GPS, DIGITAL MAPS AND COMPUTERS

Off-Road Goes High Tech

Let's face it, time is always short, and we don't want to burn daylight trying to find the trailhead or get lost once we get there. We are going to review digital map options to be used for both trip planning and finding the perfect trail.

When I first starting using GPS with computers and software, it was for search and rescue back around 2002. I had *Maptech Terrain Navigator Pro* CD's running in a *Panasonic Toughbook* Laptop through a 110-volt power converter with a NMEA feed coming from my GPS receiver through a DB-9 connector for Real-Time Tracking. Now about every device has a GPS chip in it so connecting a remote receiver is no longer necessary.

I would like to say things have become simpler since then, or have they? At least my old-school system didn't require internet or cell coverage to work. Maps have never been better than they are now with mapping technology changing at a rapid pace. The trick is to understand the pros and cons of each option so you can take advantage of the latest technology based upon your application.

Cell Apps and *Google Earth*

In the previous chapter we covered using vehicle-based GPS receivers. In this chapter we are going to cover how to trip plan and enhance using your receiver by uploading additional data as well as supplementing this information with additional app data provided on cell phones and tablets.

Using apps and computers has a high-tech cool factor. But, more importantly, it is good to take advantage of the information available to find new trails, then analyze the terrain to see what you are getting yourself into. Satellite and 3-D mapping gives flat maps new life and apps and computers allow you to take advantage of this technology.

Terrain Analysis looks at topographical maps to study the contour lines and other terrain features. These lines will give you an idea of steep grades, possible water features and other potential obstacles for driving into and out of an area. Map tools also allow you to save waypoints, mark paths and measure distances.

A huge advantage of using apps is the new ability to learn about trails through crowdsourced feedback from app users that have been there before you, rating and commenting on trails.

Real app users provide ratings and feedback on various aspects of the trip from trail difficulty to what to look for along the way. This information is critical for trip planning to understand if your truck can make the trip based upon the difficultly rating, what to bring and what to look for along the way.

Joshua Provence

Using big tablets are temping but can overheat quickly in vehicles.

Cell Phones, Tablets and Laptops

Cell phones are used for everything else, why not navigation too? Well, they do work great for street level navigation if you have a cradle to secure the phone in while driving. *Google Maps* works great in finding locations and address, then providing accurate turn-by-turn directions until you lose cell coverage.

One advantage to using a cell phone is the many off-road and hiking crowdsourced apps available that provide information from users on trails all around the world. These apps work great in Wi-Fi and are unreliable at best in cell-only range. Once you get beyond cell coverage, they don't work at all unless you were successful at downloading the map area you want to explore while you still had internet coverage.

Tablets make more sense with screens big enough to see. But, most people don't use cell phone plans with them, so once again, you are limited to what map data you can download while using Wi-Fi.

Cell phone-based apps provide more information on trails than has ever been available before, but remember you must save the map data while within Wi-Fi range. If not, the apps will not work once out of cell range.

Joshua Provence

Cell based apps are perfectly useful until cell coverage runs out.

Off-Road Mobile Apps

Mobile apps have changed the digital map landscape considerably. A number of old school mapping companies have been knocked out of the market by these cell phone-based travel apps. Lots of options to choose from for street and off-road navigation. One of the primary advantages of these apps is crowd-sourced feedback on the trails they feature.

This includes comments and photos to give you an excellent idea of what to expect once you turn off the pavement, like if your vehicle is capable to tackle the terrain to make it back out safely.

They all work great with a huge exception: they need cell coverage to work. This means if you are traveling into an area with no cell coverage (that includes most off-road areas), you must download the map area in advance while you have Wi-Fi. Here is an example of some of the more popular apps:

AllTrails

A popular off-road and hiking app that provides user ratings and feedback for each trail, free or paid subscription.
www.alltrails.com

Reviewing comments on a trail is a great way of doing trip planning.

Apple Maps

This is the map icon seen as a free factory app for iPhones. Works great most of the time for street navigation. Data from *Tom Tom* and other sources.

Backcountry Navigator Topo Maps

Downloadable topo maps for Android, free or paid subscription.
http://backcountrynavigator.com/about

Cartotracks

Downloadable topo maps for Android and Apple, free or paid subscription. Includes sites for tourism and shopping.
https://www.cartotracks.com

Backcountry Navigator used on Darin's Samsung phone.

CartoTracks provided the mapping for King of the Hammers.

Aaron Paris, Adventure Motors in Kansas City

Hema Explorer is used on an iPad Pro 10 in a Ram mount.

Hema Explorer
Downloadable topo maps for Apple, $16.95 for app.
https://www.hemamaps.com

Gaia GPS
Downloadable topo maps for Android and Apple, free or paid subscription. One of the most popular programs.
https://www.gaiagps.com

Garmin
inReach is their program for using smart phones and tablets with maps through their *Earthmate* app. For a paid subscription service, GPS data can be transferred and shared to a map so others can see your route and location. Text messages can be sent and received globally, and the receivers can also be used to send an SOS-like emergency location beacon. https://explore.garmin.com/en-US/inreach

Garmin Express is used to register and update individual GPS units.
https://www.garmin.com/en-US/software/express

Once you download *Garmin Express*, proceed to download *Garmin Basecamp*. This app allows you to download 2-D and 3-D topo, street and satellite images to your computer and manage your waypoint, track log and route data, free and paid content.
https://www.garmin.com/en-US/shop/downloads/basecamp

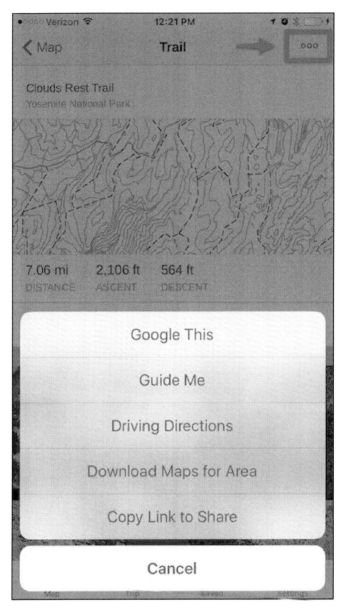

Once you have a trail to explore, you can use your default street-level navigation program for directions to get there.

Google Maps

Downloadable or free factory-installed for Android and Apple phones. Works great most of the time for street navigation. They are the go-to for determining routes and distances from location, address or city, also a great way to double check your GPS receiver if you have doubts of where it is taking you.

Another huge advantage to Google Maps is the ability to save map areas for off-line use. Default is street navigation, but toggle between Terrain (topo) or Satellite view and you have a great, free, off-road map. Tap the menu stack in the upper left-hand corner then the 'For You' square in the lower right corner. You will have an option to zoom in and out to save a map area. www.maps.google.com

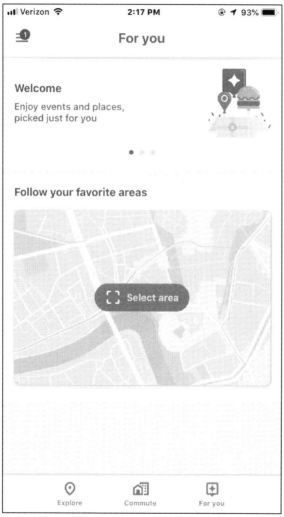

Little known fact is that you can save Google Map areas for off-line use. Toggle over to satellite view and you have a great free off-road map. Just remember to save maps with Wi-Fi before you venture out.

iOverland
Downloadable topo maps for iPhone or Android, free, donation supported. http://ioverlander.com

Lead Nav Systems

This is a more advanced map system gaining popularity among the off-road racing crowd. The system works on Apple products, providing excellent maps, satellite images and edit tools to make waypoints and routes come alive with icons, arrows and voice audible directions. Most off-roaders use iPads that are approximately 10 to 11 inches in size with many ruggedized cases available. Interestingly enough, not all *iPads* include a GPS antenna, so an external one may be needed.

Basic app is $20 but to use it to its full capacity requires a $150 pro subscription to obtain GPS capable satellite imagery. This system can also provide worldwide communication and tracking through integrated *Iridium* sat-phone communication systems.
https://leadnavsystems.com

Race team 6129 using Lead Nav on an Apple iPad to finish the 2019 Best in the Desert Vegas to Reno Race.

2019 VEGAS TO RENO

$ 25.00

Qty

1

Add to Cart

SHARE:

Lead Nav Systems provided a fully enhanced map for the Best in the Desert Vegas to Reno race complete with hundreds of voice audible directions and warnings.

Lowrance Insite Maps
Marine charts and tops maps available on SD cards or Lowrance GPS receivers. https://www.lowrance.com/lowrance/type/mapping

Motion X GPS
Downloadable topo maps and marine charts for Apple, free or paid subscription. https://gps.motionx.com

Navigon
Downloadable topo maps for Apple, free or paid subscription. Includes North America, Europe, Australia and New Zealand. Paid subscription only. https://www.navigon.com/en/mobile-app

Topo Maps
Downloadable topo maps for Android and Apple, free or paid
subscription. https://www.topomapsus.com

Topo Zone
Free digital PDF version USGS topo maps. www.topozone.com

Trails Off-Road
Downloadable topo maps for Android and Apple, free or paid
subscription. https://www.trailsoffroad.com

Wase.com by Google
Street navigation app supported by fellow users offering best routes to
take to avoid accidents and construction. Even a carpool option.
www.wase.com

 **Google Maps works great to provide topo and satellite
mapping for free. It just requires saving the map area
while in Wi-Fi.**

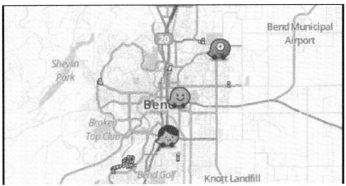

*Great for street navigation, Wase.com users can see other users and
post helpful data like, accidents, construction and ticket traps.*

 **Remember smart phone navigation apps don't work once
you are out of cellular range. You need to 'fetch all the
map tiles' you are planning to use while still in Wi-Fi.**

Using GPS with Computer Data

What make GPS receivers even more useful is the ability to upload
map data that is made or purchased, allowing you to use the most
current and customized data possible. Map waypoints and route data
can be custom-made from on-line sites such as *Google Earth* and
GPS Visualizer.

Popular off-road trail areas can be purchased through companies like *Rugged Routes*. Once data is in your GPS, you can also upload it back to a computer to analyze and share. We will take a closer look at these options.

Desert Turtle Racing

Rugged Routes provides popular off-road area maps from Glamis Dunes, Moab, and Baja ready to load into Lowrance GPS receivers.

Trip Planning with Computers and Google Earth

Google Earth is hard to beat. The price is right. Free, and it has detail the world's top spies would kill for prior to Google making their program available to the public. *Google Earth* also allows you to save, name and edit points of interest that provide coordinates and elevation. There are also map tools that let you to mark roadways and measure distances.

This platform is ideal for getting a great overview of where you want to go. Plus, you can plan your trip with amazing detail that have not been available before. Do a search of the area you are interested in. Then save the maps in a file folder.

Imagery Date: 7/15/2016   42°44'11.85" N 119°52'45.03" W elev 4646 ft

Google Earth allows you to save waypoints or points of interest. Saving an area will provide the coordinates and elevation. The default icon is a yellow pin that can be changed to various options.

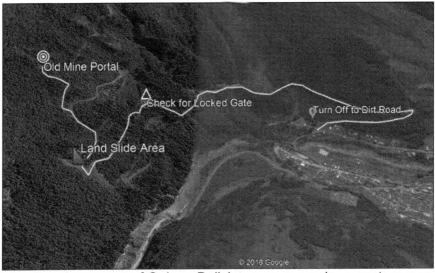

Using the above map of Quime, Bolivia as an example, a custom map on Google Earth was created to show the route from the town to an old mineshaft. The first Point Of Interest (POI), Is the location to turn off the main street to the dirt access road, (marked with a red pin). Click the 'path' icon. You can select a color and style for the path. Left click to add, right click to remove. Use the wheel on the mouse to zoom in and out. Zooming in allows you to more accurately place path or track points along a desired route.

The next POI is a gate location saved with a caution triangle. The third POI is a landslide warning area saved with a landslide icon and then finally the mine portal saved with a target icon.

Once the map is complete, title it and save it to your desktop as well as your *Google* Map folder for the specific location. Google Map's file format is KML. Once the file is saved, Google will convert it to a compressed title with under a KMZ file format.

Quime to Lost Mine

Google Earth files will save as a KML then compressed as a KMZ file labeled with the title you save them under.

Transferring Google Earth Data into GPS Receivers

Once your custom *Google Earth* map is created and saved, it is time to convert it to use in your GPS receiver. Unfortunately, these data files are not universal and will need to be converted by another software converter program. The *Google* KML/KMZ file will need to be converted into a GPX file for *Garmin* or a USR file for *Lowrance*.

To convert the Google files to GPX for Garmin use a website such as www.kml2gpx.com. To convert Google files to USR for Lowrance use a website such as www.gpsvisulizer.com. Once the files are converted drag them on to a micro SD card to install on your GPS receiver. Other conversion programs include www.expertgps.com and www.gpsbabel.org.

 Map files are relatively easy to transfer although the file extensions are different for *Google Earth, Lowrance* and *Garmin*. Fortunately, these GPS data files can be easily converted and saved with free websites.

Transferring Data Back to a GPS Receiver

So, you have found the perfect trail and saved the track log into your GPS. You even took the time to save waypoints for the trailhead and the impressive points of interest along the way. After a perfect day of off-roading you can't wait to see where you have been on good map and share with your friends. No problem, it is easier than you think. *Google Earth* will let you upload Waypoints, Tracks and Routes.

Step one, locate the map on your receiver. For example, on Lowrance, look under Waypoints, Routes and Tracks. Hit the menu button to title and save the map on your receiver's micro SD card. You can also transfer data from your GPS with a data cable.

Step two, insert the memory card or data cable into your computer and find the file. Remember, Lowrance will save a USR file and Garmin will save a GPX file. Either file will have to be saved as a KML file to upload to *Google Earth*.

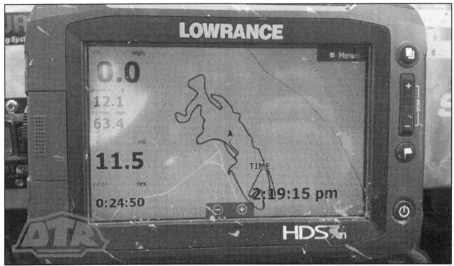

Desert Turtle Racing

Track logs and Waypoints can be easily converted and uploaded to Google Earth to analyze and share with others.

Step three, load the USR or GPX file into a file converter such as one of four previously mentioned. Select 'Keyhole Markup Language' (KML) and save.

Step four, find the saved file on your computer and right-click on it (for PC) to open with *Google Earth*. Once you select, be patient, it could take a few minutes to upload and open.

Step five, look in *Google Earth's* 'Temporary Folder' for your newly saved file. Find the new file and expand by clicking the arrow to the left. Rename and then from the File menu, save to 'My Places.'

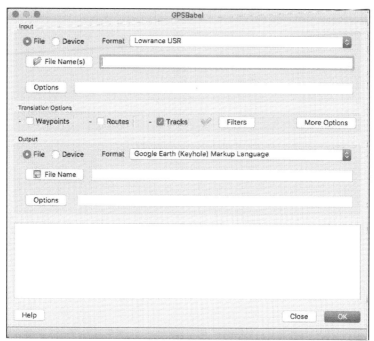

GPS Babel

To transfer your GPS created map into Google Earth, select the current file and then the output to convert to Keyhole Markup Language (KML).

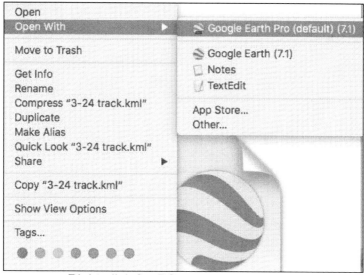

Right click for PC to open your newly saved KML file with Google Earth.

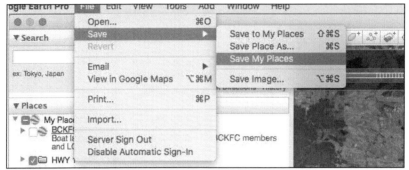

Rename your saved file, then under the
File menu, save to "My Places."

High tech doesn't replace paper maps. Large HD
screens showing amazing HD mapping is best, but it
doesn't hurt to carry low tech paper maps as a backup.

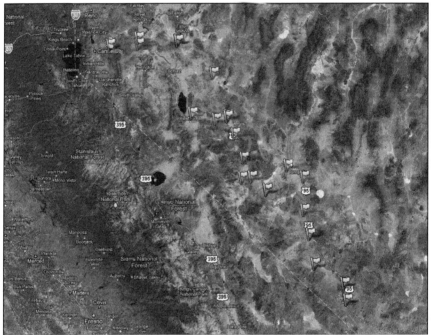

Off-Road One

GPS data uploaded to Google Earth looks great and
it is easy to share. This map shows the checkpoints
for the Vegas to Reno desert race.

This map was made by Expedition X Off-Road tours using a Lowrance and transferring data back and forth to Google Earth using GPS Babel.

Don't let your screens distract you to the point where they become a serious hazard. Have your passenger help you monitor the maps so you can keep your eyes on the road.

—	Baja 500 Course		
●	Race Mile	●	Checkpoint
○	VCP	○	Begin Speed Zone
○	BFG Pits	●	End Speed Zone

Pizza Management

This map uses color-coded waypoints for the SCORE Baja 500.

The Least you Need to Know

- Cell apps and *Google Earth* are the perfect accessory for off-road trip planning.

- Cell apps provide user ratings and feedback to help you find the perfect trail your truck is capable of driving on.

- Cell apps provide amazing map detail and user information, but will not work once out of cell range unless you saved the map area in advance while in Wi-Fi.

- *Google Earth's* detail allows for trip planning and terrain analysis anywhere in the world.

- Through the use of GPS file conversion websites, custom *Google Earth* mapping and GPS receiver data can be easily transferred back and forth.

- Do not let computer screens and high-tech mapping distract you to the point where you cause an accident. Keep focused on driving and let your passenger assist with the navigation.

16. COMMUNICATION, TRACKING, WI-FI

Communication is Everything

Can you hear me now? If you are somewhere in the middle of nowhere, probably not. Not unless you bring proper communication gear with you. The right communication equipment is critical for keeping in contact with others within your group as well as the outside world.

Besides radios, we will also look at vehicle tracking, APRS, emergency personal locator beacons and how to access Wi-Fi when traveling in and outside of cell phone range.

Me using mobile VHF radios while training with Indian Special Forces, Himalayan Mountains, India.

Options for Out-Back Communication

The following include the basics, as well as the pros and cons of each communication option.

CB Radio

Citizen Band radios have been standard equipment for off-road vehicles since the 1970's. They are low cost, easy to use and no license is required for operation. They work best for use in vehicles traveling in a convey.

This is because their four-watt transmission power output limit greatly reduces the effective communication range. Under ideal conditions, CB radio signals can travel for possibly up to ten miles, but the typical operation range is one to five miles.

The problem is the frequency range used, 26.965 to 27.405 MHz, has a poor radio wave propagation. This means the ground wave signal fails to travel very far. This is especially true in wilderness and mountainous areas where it seems these signals strain to carry a mile. The good news is that police and emergency personnel may monitor the emergency channel number nine. For best results, be sure the antenna's standing wave is adjusted to a ratio of 1:1.

Price: $50 to $150

Pro: Low cost and convenient.
                 Easy to use with no license required.
                 Emergency personnel may monitor channel nine.

Con: May not work in wilderness areas beyond one mile.

Application: Ideal use is by vehicles who travel in a group.

JL Wrangler Forums.com

CB radios have been the go-to for off-road communication for years. Their 4-watt limitation reduces their range and best used in convoys.

Cellular Phone

Cell phones are great and everyone already has one. The other benefit is that in the United States phones are GPS chipped for the Enhanced 911 feature.

This should allow the 9-1-1 operator to obtain your Latitude/Longitude coordinates. The problem, however, is that in remote areas, cell coverage can still be quite poor. If you are trying to get away from it all, chances are your phone will too, and not have service.

As covered in a previous chapter, there are a number of great off-road navigation apps, but again they will not work unless you have planned ahead to fetch the needed map data before you get out of Wi-Fi and cell range. With all those apps running your battery could go quickly, too, if not plugged in to a charger.

Price: $60 to $1,300

Pro: Most likely to already have one.
                Lots of great Off-Road trail apps.
                Low cost and convenient.
                Easy to use.
                Enhanced 911 GPS feature.

Con: Poor or no coverage in remote or wilderness areas
                Possible short battery life.

Application: If you have a cell phone, no reason not to take it along and hope for coverage. Reception can be improved, even in poor coverage areas, by attempting to place a call in higher elevation areas.

 Cell phones are convenient because everyone already has one, but don't rely on them for communication sometimes just miles outside of a metro area.

Family Radio Service (FRS) Radio

The FCC created FRS in 1996 as a part of Citizen Band radio. Fourteen channels are provided from the UHF frequencies of 465.5625 to 467.7125 MHz. The service is basically useless for backcountry applications due to its low half-watt limitation. Do not expect the range to carry more than a mile, two under ideal line-of-sight conditions.

Price: $40 to $80

Pro: Low cost and convenient.
                Easy to use and no license required.

Con: Only .5 watt.
                May not work in wilderness areas beyond one mile.
                Dependent on batteries.

Application: Close range communication only. Great to give to kids
                to use around the camp site.

General Mobile Radio Service (GMRS) Radio

The FCC created GMRS in 1983. It includes 15 channels, seven of which are FRS frequencies. The primary advantage is that these radios have four watts of power. This provides an effective communication range up to five miles, and transmissions tend to be clearer than Citizen's Band frequencies.

As of September 2017, the FCC is now requiring a license in the U.S. because radios transmit over two watts. No exam but a $75 licensing fee, good for ten years.

Price: $65 to $100

Pro: Low cost, easy to use.
                4 watts of power with a range up to 16 miles based
                upon ideal line-of-sight conditions.
Con: May not work in wilderness areas beyond one mile.
                Dependent on batteries.

Application: Primarily close-range communications only.

VHF/UHF Amateur 'Ham' Radio

The practical choice for off-road travel is using a 50 to 110-watt, vehicle mounted VHF radio. The VHF radio frequency has a longer wavelength that will travel farther with less interference.

UHF works great too, but its shorter wavelength makes it more susceptible to interference and is best used for shorter range applications. VHF radios have two major advantages over other forms of communication. The first is that mobile or vehicle can have 50 watts of power. Handheld radios typically have 5 watts of power.

Fifty watts is also enough power to punch a signal out for miles, possibly over 30 to 50 miles or more based upon line-of-site. Over 50 miles of range is not necessary for convoy travel, but it's nice to have if you need to reach civilization.

Darin Record's VHF/UHF Yaesu FTM-400XDR.

VHF radios are the top pick for off-road communication. It is not a big deal to get your entry level Technical Class amateur radio license. $15 and 35 multiple-guess questions and it is good for 10 years. ARRL.ORG

The second advantage is that transmissions can be rebroadcast over repeaters on mountain tops that allow effective communications over many more miles. Many mountain areas have ham repeaters mounted on top of them. You need to know the repeater frequency to rebroadcast your transmission.

For example, *BF Goodrich* supports race support pits in Baja, Mexico. Their main channel is 153.395 and their repeater channel is 151.715. Shouting from the mountain tops can extend an operating range over 100 miles based upon conditions and terrain. Repeaters give even 5-watt radios impressive range.

Due to the power output, in the U.S., the FCC requires a license to use. Honestly, the U.S. FCC's website and rules are confusing, but fortunately, HAM guys are happy to assist you. I am going to break this down into two sets of VHF bands:

Amateur HAM bands are 144-148 MHz
A license is required that includes a 35-question multiple-guess exam. The exam is administered by an official amateur radio volunteer typically associated with a local HAM radio club. The test is not too difficult, and much easier since the requirement to know Morse Code.

Passing the entry-level test gets you amateur Technician Class radio privileges. The cost for the license is $15 for ten years. You will get your own call sign that you can bring down to your DMV office to get your own call sign license plates.

Commercial/Business bands are 150-174 MHz
Most off-road racing and event radio traffic uses this band range. Considering these bands are designated for commercial use, a HAM license is not required, but a Private Land Mobile Radio (PLMR) license is required. No exam is needed, and no call sign too. The licensing cost is $70 for five years.

The Multi-Use Radio Service, (MURS) also operates within these bands and no license is required if the operator uses less than 2 watts of transmission. Even if you only plan on using the Commercial/Business bands, it is still a good idea to get a full HAM license.

In the backcountry, you might find there is more traffic and repeaters in the HAM bands that could be the advantage you need to find assistance. Also, a HAM license covers the Commercial/Business bands, so you are not required to carry two different licenses.

Price: $150 to $700

Pro: 50 watts for mobile radios.
              Use of repeaters greatly extends effective
              communications range.

Con: Requires FCC licensing and fees.

Application: Ideal for mobile or handheld backcountry communication.

Satellite Phone

Who needs cell towers when you can use satellites and chat anywhere in the world? I thought we would all be using sat phones by now for everyday use, but we are not there yet. Just as implied by the name, these phones rely on satellite transmission instead of individual ground-based cell towers. This provides the ability to talk, text, send photos, even Skype about anywhere on the planet.

Nate Hunt from BF Goodrich Racing demos their sat phone system capable of making private calls to group push-to-talk, PTT broadcasts.

BF Goodrich Racing   PCI Race Radios

Satellite phone antennas extend and improve reception,
ideal for comms up and down the Baja Peninsula.

Satellite phones are ideal for serious backcountry or developing country use. They are not cheap, but if you need to communicate, it's worth it. Ideally the technology will improve, and these sat comm systems will be become more accessible and affordable.

Price: $600 to $1,200 per phone. $5,000 to $6,000 for vehicle mount systems with handset, MSAT base and remote antenna. Phones can be rented or leased. Airtime is approximately $1.00 per minute.

Pro: Easy to use like a cell phone with nearly complete global coverage. Includes the ability to text, send photos, PTT broadcasting, *Skype,* and internet access.

Con: Expensive, but electronics and airtime should become more affordable.

Application: Ideal for international travel, especially in remote areas and developing countries.

For more information and products visit our friends at *Ham Radio Outlet*, www.hamradio.com

GPS Based Tracking

Automatic Position Reporting System (APRS)

Amateur radio buffs have been using this tracking system since 1992. APRS uses a GPS and VHF radio frequencies to broadcast and track one's position. A terminal node controller (TNC), is used to digitize GPS coordinates in the NMEA format for radio transmission. Software decodes these digital transmissions to display the tracked object's location on a computer screen's map.

The primary national designated frequencies for this transmission are on VHF 144.390, on UHF 445.925 and 144.800 in Europe.

The APRS system is made up of mobile stations such as persons or vehicles being tracked. This can range from search dogs to helicopters, nearly anyone or anything that a receiver and radio can be attached to. Mobile stations being tracked show as the user's call sign with a number code behind it, such as 9 to indicate it's a vehicle, for example, KD7PAY-9. A '3' at the end indicates it's a handheld tracker.

The location of objects can be entered manually, such as for tracking tornadoes. You will also see stationary base and weather stations (WX) symbol, appearing on a map. The basis of an APRS station is a GPS signal in NMEA format, going into a Terminal Node Controller (TNC), which works as a modem. The digital GPS data is then broadcast through the VHF radio. The APRS software allows the radio to receive and display packets of information and location data from other APRS users so they can be displayed on a map.

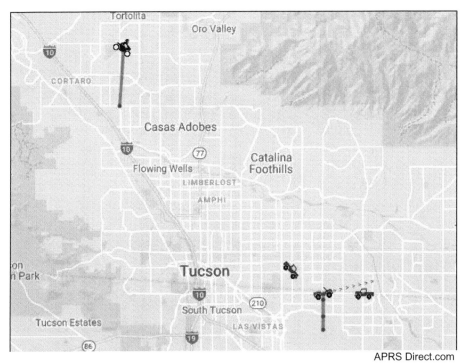

APRS Direct.com

Websites such as APRSdirect.com and APRS.fi show stationary, weather and mobile APRS users.

It is obvious to see how useful APRS can be. From keeping track of other off-road vehicles on the trail to tracking off-road race cars to search and rescue emergency management.

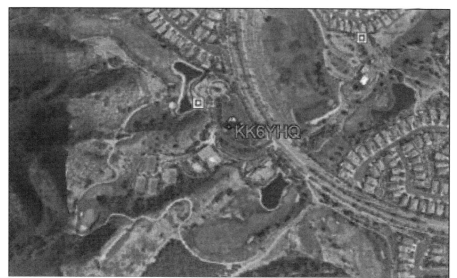

Here is a vehicle smart enough to leave the suburbs for the mountains displayed on APRS.fi using a Google Earth map layer.

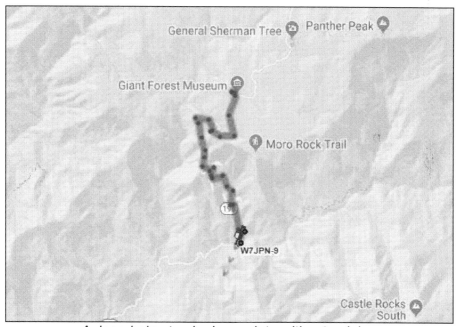

A Jeep being tracked complete with a track log showing its path on APRSDirect.com

Do not let the screens and dials distract you from driving. Let your passenger assist you with your communication and tracking so the driver can keep their eyes and attention on the road.

231

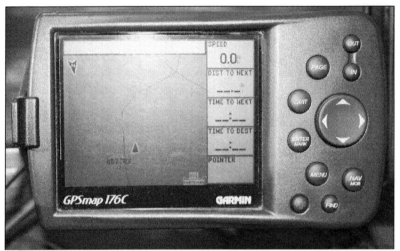

A Kenwood TM A700D with a built-in TNC and APRS firmware provides a Garmin 176C with the location of a nearby friend represented by his radio call sign.

This is a portable APRS pack I set up using a Kenwood THD7A handheld with built-in TNC cabled into a Garmin GPS. It was used for search and rescue, attaching it to support vehicles from volunteer Jeeps, snow mobiles, even a K9 tracker.

Honestly, last two *Kenwood* and *Garmin* GPS examples are old school. Systems I used 10-15 years ago, but so goes the way of APRS.

It is outdated, clunky homemade cables and often a cumbersome miss-mash of technology and software. When you see it working however, there is a sense of amazement that this old technology provides, capable of impressing even the highest of high-tech geeks.

Dual band radios are ideal because one channel is used for voice communication and the second band use reserviced to broadcast and receive APRS data. Recent innovations include streamlining the process by *Kenwood* and *Yaesu* with radios with built-in TNCs and GPS. Then a data out cable is used with a NMEA format and 9600 baud rate settings to display the APRS users being tracked.

This most durable option is having it display on a chart plotter style GPS receiver where you can travel anywhere without the need to download maps. The second option is using a PC tablet connected by a USB cable or Bluetooth.

Live tracking can be done on PC tablets using *APRSDroid.org* software. Even better, *APRSDroid* can be used in conjunction with the *Android* app, *Backcountry Navigator*. This is ideal for showing the vehicles you want to keep track of on an off-road navigation app you would use anyway. Others have set up *Windows* tablets using *APRSIS32* software, but it appears this has not been updated since 2012? Unfortunately, it does not seem like there is a similar option for *Apple* products.

Kenwood TM-D710G with built in TNC and GPS.
Their handheld counterpart is the Kenwood TH-D72A.

Yaesu FTM-400XDR with built-in TNC and GPS.
Their handheld counterpart is the Yaesu FT-2DR C4FM.

W2APRS

W2APRS provides software for Android devices
to show tracking data on Google Maps.

 As clunky and potentially outdated, APRS remains extremely useful and amazingly cool to watch it work.

The APRS.FI website is popular to find APRS stations. They also offer the only updated and supported app for iPhones and iPads.

For more information on amateur radio use and APRS checkout:

Bob Bruninga's page (the inventor of APRS)   www.aprs.org

ARRL American Relay League   www.arrl.org

Racing TraX.com

Racing TraX is a satellite-based tracking and communication system designed for off-road motorsports. Spectators can log into the system on their smart phones and search for any car number or race class to receive an update on the status of the car(s). Status includes speed and location and is updated every eight minutes.

From the race car, driver and co-driver can see the location of chase vehicles as well as communicate with them via satellite text. They can also send alerts that include: medical, mechanical, if emergency stopped or a request to pass. Case teams can see the location of the race car and other case personnel as well as send and receive text messages.

This system can even sense if the race car has crashed or rolled over, sending an emergency message to race rescue HQ. These features substantially increase safety in this form of extreme off-road racing.

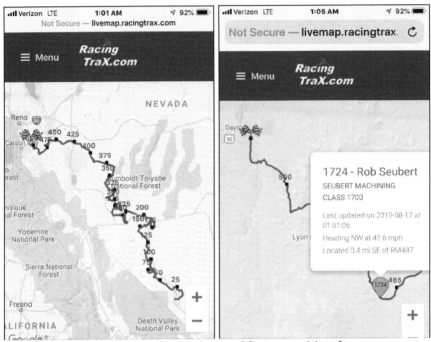

Racing TraX shows the mile markers for the 505 mile, 2019 Vegas to Reno desert race

After searching for a car, we can see the exact location and speed on the course.

Racing TraX LED monitor on the dash of the 6129 truck.

Other options for GPS, Vehicle Based Tracking

Garmin Rino

If your navigation, communication and tracking needs are close-range localized, the *Garmin Rino* system could be ideal. GPS, radio, APRS all combined in one compact package. These units are great for trail runs, exploring, camping, hunting, search & rescue and many other activities where you want to keep in contact and track of your outdoor friends with the bonus of having a premier GPS receiver included.

Garmin developed the Rino receiver to combine GPS with FRS/ GMRS radio. These units transmit digital coordinate information allowing receivers within range to appear on each other's screen.

GMRS radio have up to four-watts of power that can provide an average up to five miles or more of range based upon line-of-site. As of September 2017, FCC is now requiring a license in the U.S. because radios transmit over two watts. No exam but a $75 licensing fee, good for ten years.

Price:　　　　Garmin 750, model $650 (earlier models for less).

Pro:　　　　Ideal for communication, navigation and training all-in-one for outdoor activities within one to five miles.

Con:　　　　May not work in wilderness areas beyond one mile. Dependent on batteries. Latest Garmin models are expensive, but earlier and used models available for much less.

Application: Excellent all-in-one until for localized outdoor activities.

LeadNav

If you manage a race team for the *Baja 1000* in Mexico or a team of mercenaries attempting to rescue a kidnapped client in South America, then *LeadNav* has the navigation, communication and tracking system for you. It is satellite-based through Iridium satellite communication so the world can be your playground.

The system is based upon the Apple iPhone and iPads with a monthly subscription fee of $204 per month. The system is also comprehensive enough to require some training by the users.

LeadNav uses iPads or iPhones for their premier navigation software.

LeadNav uses military grade products with iPhones or iPads.
Custom prepared packages are designed for your unique application.

Price: Thousands for custom prepared packages with custom
                mapping based upon your application plus monthly
                service fees up to $204.

Pro: Ideal for communication, navigation and training all-in-
                one for outdoor activities anywhere on the globe.

Con: Priced for pro users. Training is also required.

Application: Excellent all-in-one unit for global outdoor operations.

For more information see www.leadnavsupply.com.

Personal Locator Beacons (PLB's)

You can take advantage of the same emergency beacon technology
that has been used in aircraft and ships for years. PLB's are the
ultimate satellite-based 9-1-1 distress alert system that can summon
search and rescue personal to your location worldwide. They are
about the size of a GPS receiver and when activated by the registered
user, the signal broadcast through a 406 MHz transmitter is received
by U.S. National Oceanic and Atmospheric Administration (NOAA)
satellites.

To avoid confusion, let's review some terminology on related
technology. Emergency Position Indicating Radio Beacon (EPIRB), is
used for boating and marine applications. Emergency Locator
Transmitter (ELT), are used in aircraft. Emergency Locator Beacons
(ELB), are used for hikers, climbers and drivers doing overland travel.

*These PLBs like the SPOT Gen 3 and the ACR PLB- 375 are
designed to send a one-time emergency rescue request.*

More advanced PLBs offer more advanced messaging and tracking features. Subscription services allow two-way text messaging and the ability for family and friends to log into a site to see your location. Garmin's InReach Explorer includes full GPS receiver capabilities.

PLB's use GPS combined with a 121.5 MHz homing signal to take the search out of search and rescue and can be used anywhere in the world. Once NOAA satellites receive a PLB signal, that data is processed and emergency alerts are routed to the Air Force Rescue Coordination Center (AFRCC), Langley Air Force Base in Virginia.

The AFRCC then forewords the data to the appropriate search and rescue agency. Depending on your location and circumstances, you could very well get a rescue bill from a private company or government agency so these should only be used in life or death emergency situation.

PLB owners must register their device with NOAA so emergency personnel know who they are going after. This data includes any special medical conditions, family contact telephone numbers and any other information that can be helpful to rescuers. If you purchase a used PLB or change your information, be sure you update your registration.

PLB's come into two different categories. The first is simple and reliable one button, one-time use to send an emergency rescue request. No subscriptions or monthly fees. You just need to make sure your device is registered and includes your emergency contact information and any medical conditions, etc.

The second option includes communication capabilities through worldwide texting.

PLB's have been greatly improved with the ability to use service plans to allow for international texting and tracking.

Family, friends and work associates can also log into your account to see your location as a way to check in on you. These services require a monthly subscription. Monthly plans vary by provider but seem to range from $12 to $60 per month depending on how many messages you want to send.

SPOT has a unique *'Save our Vehicle, SOV'* program where you can request roadside assistance for your truck, ATV or RV, when if there is no road. They partner with towing and repair companies that can help you even if you are off-road for $30 per year. I'm sure that you would also get a bill for the off-road rescue that would be much more than that, but what a great idea and a way to have peace of mind that you will not be stranded.

Price: $250 to $400 USD retail. Some outfitters offer rental programs to make them more affordable. Monthly service plans for worldwide texting and tracking will vary between $12 and $60 per month based upon usage.

Pro: Easy to use one-button wilderness 9-1-1 call for help worldwide. Texting allows you to check in with civilization without hitting the panic button.

Con: Can be expensive and relies on batteries.

Application: Ideal for any remote and international travel.

Wi-Fi on the Road

Staying in a van down by the river becomes easier if you can maintain contact with the outside world. We may want to create a mobile office or have access to our favorite streaming entertainment. To do all of that you have a few options, but unfortunately not as many as you think. As high-tech as our world is, you would think by now we could have fast, low-cost satellite-based Wi-Fi anywhere on the planet. Sadly, that's not the case.

Here is a look at what technology is available now to keep connected:

Cell Phone Extenders
Cell phone extenders boost cell coverage you already have. Distance from cell towers as a well as terrain features weaken cellular signals.

The high gain antenna and amplification system of these systems can provide enough signal to prevent dropped calls in many remote areas.

WeBoost by *Wilson Amplifiers* is the main brand. They make a car/truck sized unit and a larger sized model for RV's. Either model can provide up to a 50 dB gain at a price of $499 each.

WeBoost Drive Reach has a 4" magnetic antenna for vehicle applications

WeBoost 4G-X OTR has a a large mast style antenna for RV's.

Price: $250 to $800 USD retail.

Pro: Usually makes the difference between dropped calls to being able to use your phone.

Con: Expensive, no guarantee it will work if too remote.

Application: Ideal for remote travel and operations like search & rescue where you need to use a cell phone.

 Understanding Wi-Fi is all about the MBPS, Megabytes Per Second. Your computer network settings can display the download and upload speed.

Wi-Fi Hotspots

Wi-Fi Hotspots are locations that you can log into that may or may not be password protected. These sites are location specific such as an office or coffeeshop. Ideally, you can create your own to take with you on your travels. The easiest way to do this is to turn your own cell phone into a hotspot through your cell phone provider's data plan.

If you have a reasonably good cell signal, you can create a hotspot to possibly check and send email on a laptop computer before driving out of cell range. This can be done through a cell phone or a 'Jet Pack' transmitter device.

FreedomPOP is a hotspot provider, up to 200 MBs free through a sim card that can go into a cell phone. That allows you to turn an old cell phone into a hotspot device with speeds up to 12 MBPS. They provide this service for free through AT&T in the hope to upsell you into a text and cell phone program.

Skyroam sells their *Solis X* Wi-Fi hotspot provides service in over 130 countries with unlimited data at $9 per day or $99 per month. This is ideal for RV'ers or international travelers who need unlimited internet access.

Skyroam provides a Wi-Fi hotspot in 130 countries around the world.

Price: Free to $100 per month USD retail.

Pro: Your smartphone can be a hotspot, or a transmitter device can be purchased cheap. Great way to do business on the road when you need a laptop.

Con: Cell data plans can get expensive. Will not work out of cell coverage.

Application: Ideal for doing business with a laptop while still in cell phone range.

Checking Your Wi-Fi Speed

Wi-Fi performance or speed is measured in MBPS, Megabytes Per Second. Your Windows 10 computer will allow you to check your Wi-Fi speed without any additional software or downloaded apps. Checking your speed is important to see if you are pulling enough signal to download or upload photos or streaming media. It is also a way to check before and after performance to Wi-Fi boosters.

How fast of Internet do you need?

• General surfing	1-2 MBPS
• Online gaming	1-3 MBPS
• Video conferencing	1-4 MBPS
• Streaming a standard definition video	3-5 MBPS
• Streaming a high-definition video	5-8 MBPS
• Up or Downloading large files	50+ MBPS

It is also useful to understand data usage to know that there are 1,000 megabytes (MBs) in one gigabyte (GBs). How many GBs would you use a month? Here is an example: Checking 200 emails, listening to 100 hours of music, 28 hours of web surfing, 30 social media posts and 20 hours of video streaming requires 8.3 GBs.

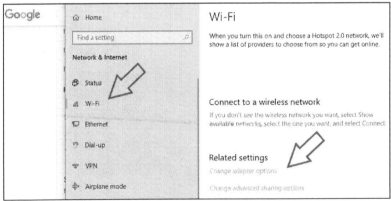

For Windows 10, search Network and Internet, highlight Wi-Fi, then select 'Change adaptor options.'

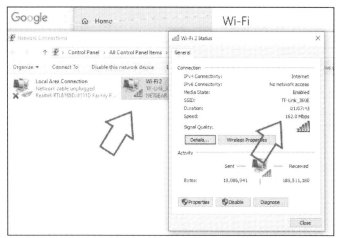

*Windows 10, highlight the Wi-Fi connection network, then
a new box will pop up showing the speed, in this case 162 MBPS.*

Wi-Fi Hotspot Boosters

Wi-Fi boosters are ideal for bringing in weak hotspots that you may already have access to from campgrounds to coffee shops. Wi-Fi boosters work similar to cell phone boosters, using a larger antenna and amplifier to make weak, distant signals usable.

There are many Wi-Fi antenna/amplifier boosters such as the highly rated *Alfa WiFi Camp Pro 2*. Another option is the *Winegard Connect 2.0 WF2-335 RV Wi-Fi Extender* with 4G LTE. The benefit of this system is that it works as a Wi-Fi booster with the option to purchase cellular data through various options or insert a sim card from your own cell phone carrier. For example, through *Winegard's FreedomGo* program, 3 GBs of data can be purchased a month for $35.

Dan Kirk

The Alfa Wi-Fi Camp Pro 2 is a highly ranked Wi-Fi extender for $150.

*Winegard Connect 2.0 RV Wi-Fi Extender provides a
Wi-Fi booster with a sim card slot to purchase monthly data.*

Price: $360 USD retail plus optional monthly data plan that
              could range from $20 to $100.

Pro: Excellent way to utilize networks already available, but
              maybe too weak to use without a booster.

Con: Bulky antennas, equipment can be expensive and
              needs to be wired, mounted on and in vehicle. No
              guarantee it will work if too remote.

Application: Ideal for staying in RV parks and other areas that
              already provide Wi-Fi, but maybe too weak to use.

Satellite Wi-Fi

Need to stay in contact and still get beyond where cell signals can
reach? Satellite may be the answer, but it is not a cheap or easy
answer. I thought by now most communication would be satellite-
based. Unfortunately, that is far from the case.

There are three companies that apparently provide satellite Wi-Fi for
RV'ers. The only company I could get information from is *RV Data
Sat*. They provide the option of two folding dish antennas that cost
$7,000 or $16,000. The monthly service plan to provide 2 MBPS
download, and 1 MBPS upload speed is $409 a month. 2 MBPS is
enough to stream movies and video, but they better be good at this
price.

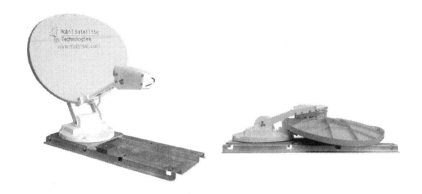

RV Data Sat folding dish antenna options, $7,000 or $16,000 to provide only a 2 MBPS download speed.

Despite the high cost and slow speeds, this system is ideal for those who need to stay connected outside of cell phone range. It will work about anywhere in North America if the antenna is pointing at the southern sky. That also means the vehicle needs to be stationary while the satellite is set facing south. Weather can disrupt service and the company can also reduce speeds during peak hours.

Price: Up to $16,000 for equipment and $409 per month service fees USD retail.

Pro: Only way to stay connected outside of cell phone range.

Con: Expensive equipment and service plans for the low connection speed.

Application: Ideal for full-time travelers who need to stay connected outside of cell phone coverage areas.

The Least You Need to Know

- CB radios were the old standby for the trail, but they have been primarily replaced with longer-range radio options like VHF.

- Cell phones are convenient except they do not work beyond cell range, which unfortunately can only be a few miles outside of town.

- VHF mobile Ham radios are ideal for off-road communication. Their power and range make them the top choice despite a license requirement.

- Satellite phones are ideal when you need to communicate beyond cell phone range.

- APRS tracking combines GPS and VHF radio providing a fun and useful way to keep track of your friends on the trail.

- Personal Locator Beacons provide a wilderness 911. What makes them even better is that service plans are available for tracking, texting, and emergency vehicle recovery.

- Cell phone extenders are great for using your cell phone beyond its normal service limits.

- Hotspots, hotspot generators and boosters provide a low-cost way of staying connected on the road.

- Satellite Wi-Fi is expensive, but it will keep you online beyond cell range.

17. OFF ROAD SURVIVAL

Outwit, Out Pack and Tell Someone Where You are Going.

As adventurers and off-road drivers, it is not unusual for us to do things a little over the top. No wonder then, when the going gets tough, we do not only want to survive-but thrive. Despite enjoying the best trucks and gear, that does not mean that somehow misfortune will escape us. Many of us drive farther and challenge ourselves and our machines far beyond what most would consider reasonable. If fact, a seriously dangerous situation is just around the next trail for a few of us. It is inevitable.

To thrive in the outdoors, you must stay healthy and know how to fix things. That means not only trucks but people too. Spend enough time in the backcountry and you will see a variety of accidents, injuries, crashes, and storms. Some of this is caused by factors difficult to anticipate or completely out of our control. Others, from complacency and failing to prepare, or from downright dangerous stupidity.

The challenge is that you just can't be prepared for everything. We can anticipate potential hazards, but life is too big and unpredictable to even try to guess what might happen next. Bring what you need, know what you must know, but I'm asking to take a page from the *Boy Scouts Handbook*, and be prepared.

Consider ever possible problem and contingency to get out of it. Meet the challenge head on and succeed. This is done two ways: one, by planning ahead, and doing the best you can to prevent obvious problems from occurring. Second, by thinking the situation through and making sound decisions until you are out of the woods-literally.

Fortunately, in vehicle-based travel, we do have an amazing amount of control. Control over the condition and capabilities of the truck we are driving. Control over the gear we bring and where we go. Also, control over our attitude, our resourcefulness and how we will respond when Murphy's Law throws the book at us. Ask yourself some serious questions as you prepare for your next adventure. Like, can you get through any of the following possible challenges?

Snake Bite	Gunshot Wound
Flat Tire	Snowstorm
Credit Card Failure	Lost Cell Phone
Getting Stuck	Minor Repair
Blown Engine	Getting Lost

73-year-old Gregory Randolph was rescued in the Oregon desert after four days. His Jeep got stuck and was lucky enough to be found by a mountain biker who had an Emergency Locator Beacon, saving Randolph's life. Could you survive without counting on luck?

Here is some good advice to help ensure that you return from every trip with a big smile on your face and lots of pictures in your camera.

Survival of the Smartest

Be aware that survival is a mental game. Those who believe they can live usually do, and those who give up, well, it may not work out so well for them. You also may need to redefine what comfort and survival means to you.

Traveling around the undeveloped world you will see people that live with and on practically nothing in extreme weather and circumstances. People survive in cold and heat, with very little food and water every day. You surviving for a day or two until rescued is not the end of the world. You might be hungry, cold, sunburned and thirsty, but it is probably not going to kill you. Honestly, being in a survival situation has a beautiful simplicity to it. Nothing else matters until you find a way to make it through.

Our ancient ancestors survived for thousands of years with no modern convivences, with maybe some stone tools in a cave. You have a well-equipped 4WD full of tools and gear-so suck it up. How did the native people survive? How did they live, eat and drink? If they can survive, with some research and training, you can too.

Survival is a mental game you learn to win. Whatever you think you need, someone else is doing it with less than half. I found this truck with three lug nuts on Bolivia's Death Road.

Plan Ahead

Remember to be a traveler and not a tourist. This is done by researching where you are going, how to get there and back, and what you will need for a successful trip. The best and most stress-free trips are from having someone with you that has local knowledge. Like using a guide or ideally travel with a group that has been there before. Check the weather so you know how to pack and don't forget any special considerations if you take children or dogs.

Tell Someone Where You Are Going

Leave behind a travel itinerary to allow someone to know where you are going, who you are traveling with, and when you are planning to return. Also, let them know if it is possible for someone to communicate with you. Like the radio frequency or satellite phone number are you using.

Pack Right

It is tricky to know how much to take with you. We often pack lots of things we don't use while forgetting the cell phone charger cord. My friend Loyd Kruse says, "More is almost always better than less and too much is just right." The best food and drink in the wilderness is what you take with you! One of the huge advantages of vehicle-based travel is you have more room to take things (compared to backpacking). You should have basic survival essentials packed with you anyway but check your packing lists to make sure you did not forget anything critical. Once I make it a mile or two past my driveway, I joke that if we forgot something, it is now up to the VISA card.

Dress for Success

I am from Oregon where honestly, we are not known for fashion sense. I am talking more about practicality than brand labels. On the same trail you will see t-shirts and snow jackets, flip flops and snow boots. It is more like people wear what they have instead of thinking about where they are going and what they are doing once they get there.

Bill Burke says, "There is no bad weather, only inappropriate gear." Long sleeves and pants are best, even in warm weather to help protect skin from the sun and elements. Bring boots with ankle support and extra socks. Wide-brim hats work great for sun and rain. Layers work great for removing and adding as needed depending on how hard you are working and the weather.

Avoid all cotton clothing, like jeans. The problem is when they get wet, it can take days to dry. Wet cotton clothing will suck the heat out of your body and can freeze. Look for travel clothes with poly-nylon blends that have lots of pockets.

Have a Way to Communicate

Two or more is even better. Cell phone, amateur radio, satellite phone, personal locator beacon, (PLB). Whichever you choose, let someone know on your travel itinerary how they can contact you in the event of an emergency.

Understand Navigation Basics

Learn the navigation basics we cover in this book. GPS yes, and the basics too, like map, compass and how to get directions from nature. Again, it is better if you can go with a guide or a group who knows where to go and what to do once you get there. Traveling in a group with an experienced guide can be more fun with less stress anyway.

Water

Water is probably the most important element for remaining healthy and comfortable. Your radiator might need water also, so there's no reason not to have at least one gallon on board and a five-gallon water can if you are camping. Drinking untreated water is very risky and can result in illness from parasites or diarrhea. Getting diarrhea will tap you of what fluids and energy you have left, only making matters worse. There are several ways to serialize water making if safe to drink: boiling, bleach, pumping through a filter or water treatment tablets.

The best food and water in the outdoors is what you take with you.

Food

The best food in the outdoors is what you take with you! Besides, cooking outdoor meals is fun and the food always tastes better than the same meal in civilization, especially if you can cook over a fire. It is helpful to bring two coolers if you have the room. One for drinks and the other for meats and other food. Having food and drinks separated keeps your drinks from floating in food contaminated melted ice water.

For quick and easy or emergency food, Meals Ready to Eat, (MRE's) and freeze-dried backpacking meals work great. Even better if supplemented with other high-calorie foods with a long shelf life. This includes power bars, nuts, jerky with canned food like stew and beans. Write the purchase date on this food with a permanent marker to be sure to eat the stuff up before it expires.

Learn what edible wild plants, berries, fruits and vegetables are available in the area you are traveling in.

If you must eat from the wildernesses' snack bar, you will need to work at maintaining the 2,500+ calories needed to keep you warm and function in the outdoors. Berries and bugs can keep you alive. Better yet, use food scraps to bait in small game at night. Your best odds of hunting is after dark as most animals are nocturnal. A slingshot or hand carved spear could score you a rabbit, squirrel, snake or fish.

Discovery Channel Treasure Quest
Cooking and eating a wild rabbit in the Sacambaya Jungle, Bolivia.

 Camp cooking is the best, but in a pinch, canned food can be warmed up quickly on the exhaust manifold of an idling engine. It is not fancy, but better than eating cold food.

Fire

Fire good. Humans have known this since the dawn of time. Fire provides warmth, cooks food, boils water and provides a signal for someone to find you. Equally important, fire provides a real psychological comfort. Anyone who as ever sat around a campfire knows there is no therapy better that 'Outback TV.'

There are several ways to get the fire blazing from a vehicle. The best way is a windproof mini-torch cigar lighter and a tube of fire-starting paste. This will get fires started even with wet material in minutes. Other options include; Cigarette lighter, waterproof matches, 12-volt plug, road flares, battery cables shorted out over fuel-soaked tissue and camera filter lens makes a good magnifying glass.

There are many ways to start a fire, but most failures are from people trying to use too large of wood. Start small, using very small twigs and other woodsy material that can more easily burn, even when wet.

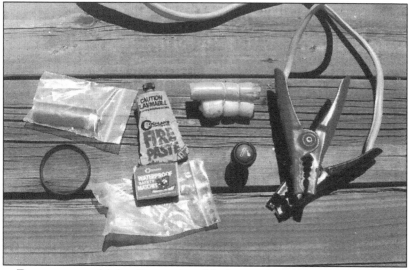

From your vehicle, there should always been several options to start a fire. A windproof cigar torch and fire paste works best.

One of the best methods of starting a fire with wet material is a candle or fire paste under a twig teepee. The rising heat helps dry out wet material.

One of the best methods is to make a twig teepee over a candle or some other burning material from fire paste to a plastic candle wrapper. The rising heat will dry out any wet materials above it. Slowly add more swigs, then sticks while blowing into the embers. Once completely burning, you can add larger pieces of wood.

Shelter

Your truck is home-sweet-home. If broken down or lost, stay with your vehicle. It will provide shelter, warmth and supplies to get you through until help arrives. Be sure to always pack a tarp. Tarps are very useful for everything from installing tire chains, working under your truck to making an awning or tent.

Shelter is very important to keep you dry and out of the elements. Staying warm and dry helps prevent hypothermia and staying out of the sun helps prevent heat exposure, two of the leading causes of outdoor-related injuries. A tarp, or large plastic trash bags and some rope or paracord can be used to easily make additional cover to supplement what your vehicle can provide.

You can make a tent in minutes with a tarp, rope and sticks for stakes. No tarp, use large trash bags and paracord. Even with snow on the ground, I had stayed reasonably warm.

Dangerous Weather

Personally, I like storms. Camping in thunder and lightning is an adventure but traveling into a blizzard or hurricane is frightening. With the technology at our fingertips like the *WeatherBug* app, there is no reason to not check the weather we might be getting into.

Here are some points to remember when you must ride the storm out:

Too Cold Hypothermia is one of the leading causes of outdoor-related injury and death. Increased wind and moisture make it worse through the *Wind Chill Factor*. Use your shelter to get out of the wind and use your heater or fire as much as you can to stay warm.

Too Wet Getting soaked can result in the rapid loss of body heat. Remove or do not use cotton clothing, it does not dry quickly. Use your shelter to improve your comfort and survivability.

Too Hot Keep covered, use shelter and keep hydrated. Take cool-off breaks with the air conditioning if possible. Exert yourself as little as possible to help keep your body temp as low as possible. Wind exposure will dehydrate you even faster.

Snowstorm If you can move, drive out of it as soon as possible. If you are stuck, collect as much firewood as possible before there is a high snow accumulation on the ground. If your vehicle is buried in the snow, be careful about continually running the engine. You will need to dig out an exhaust exit, or carbon dioxide gasses could enter your vehicle and asphyxiate you.

High Wind In extreme high wind you will need to take down your roof top tent, tarps, awnings and pop up shelters as soon as possible. Wind gusts can destroy all these fabric shelters in seconds. I have failed to take mine down, and it is an expensive mistake. You need to take hard shelter (like in your truck) and sit it out.

Thunder & Lighting Stay in your vehicle and keep the windows rolled up. Your tires will provide you some insolation. Stay put until 30 minutes after the last strike. Stay off hill tops, open areas, bodies of water or tall objects. Get to low ground and take cover as you do not want to be the tallest object in a lightning storm, especially on foot.

 Check the weather with apps like *Weather Bug* to see what you are getting into before you leave. This will also help you pack and know what to wear.

Dangerous Animals and Plants

OK sure, in your vehicle you are safe, but if you get out in the wilderness, you could run across an unfriendly animal or find yourself deep in poison oak. Fortunately, most four-legged predator animals will go out of their way to avoid humans.

Bears can be spooked by noise and cougars can be spooked by you looking larger and more menacing. If you run across a predator, back out slowly without running. Running makes you look like dinner and they may chase you.

As far as the creepy-crawly, watch where you are placing your hands and feet. Insects like mosquitos are typically more troublesome than any other creatures. Always watch where you are walking as well as check your sleeping bag, clothing, and boots before slipping into them.

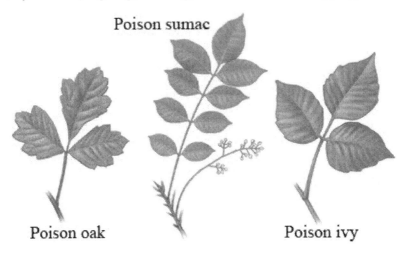

Learn what poison oak and ivy look like and stay away from them. Wear pants and long-sleeved clothing and use insect repellent. I used *Deet* on my bandana to help keep from being bit by potentially Yellow Fever mosquitos in the jungles of Bolivia. *Benadryl* cream and pills can help with the symptoms from poison leaves, stings, and bites.

Carry a first aid kit that includes a snakebite kit. Venomous snakes have broad heads to contain their venom sacks on each side, behind their jaws. Also, venomous snakes have fangs instead of rows of teeth. If bit by a snake, *Diazepam* or *Valium* can help slow the heart rate to prevent the venom from spreading through the bloodstream. Carry a first aid guide with a well-packed first aid kit. Better yet, have a first responder join you on your expedition.

Keep your clothes and boots zipped up in your tent.
A tarantula I found in the Sacambaya Jungle, Bolivia.

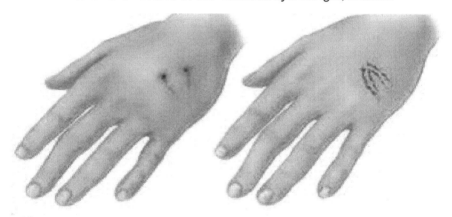

Venomous snakes have fangs that leave two puncture holes (left).
Nonvenomous snakes tend to have rows of teeth (right).

Dangerous People

Most people you meet in the outdoors are friendly and would go out of their way to help you. There is a very small percentage whose intentions are unclear. Maybe they are opportunists who might steal your gear or mess with you if they really felt they could get away with it. An even smaller percentage of people are downright outlaws. They use the woods to hide out and for illegal dumping or drug operations.

If you run across someone or a group who may be unfriendly, are asking too many questions or you feel like they cannot be trusted, the best thing to do is just leave. If you run across a drug operation or criminal activity, carefully and quietly back out and leave. This is important because fighting in a remote area on their turf is extremely risky and unpredictable. You don't know how many unfriendlies there may be or what weapons they have. If you are approached by one or two, they could be feeling you out for the dozen around the corner.

 There are many ways to defend yourself with the tools you already have. The best weapons don't look out of place when you are holding them in the outback, like machetes, shovels, axes and tire irons.

Jens Stoermer

No shortage of potentially dangerous people in every country in the world. Tib Bardai bandits in Libya.

Many countries, like in South America, have turned kidnapping for ransom into an industry. If you must travel or work in potentially hostile areas, hire local security to assist you. Let them carry the weapons or firearms to protect you. Picking up and possessing firearms in most countries outside the United States will probably land you in jail regardless if you are defending yourself or someone else.

If you find yourself in a situation where you must defend yourself through a fight, do it as if your life and the lives of those with you depend on it.

If in a country where picking up a firearm will get you shot or in jail, hire local security. They know who's who and what are the best options to protect you. Me and one of our guards in Bolivia.

Even if you might have to explain yourself to authorities or take another person's life, the goal is to survive the encounter until you can retreat out of harm's way and get help.

Whether you have access to firearms or security, there should be tools all around you that can be used for defense. The best tools are the ones you should have already that don't look out of place when they are in your hand when being approached. Like a machete, axe or shovel. Many hikers carry pepper or bear spray that is non-lethal and is very effective against humans and animals. Again, something that doesn't look out of place attached to your belt or pack but can be very useful when you need it most.

Be resourceful, I once used a tire iron out of a rental car to get out of a potentially tricky inner-city standoff in L.A. Know that criminals like easy targets. It could be like a business for them, and they need to manage risk, too. They typically do not want to mess with people who look aware, confident, and capable of defending themselves. Act like you are not afraid and willing to fight like you have nothing to lose. A fight provides the reality that if you win, you get through it, if you lose, things could go from bad to fatal. Choose to survive by stepping up when you need to protect yourself and those with you.

 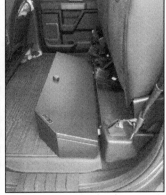

Mauriziopecoraro.com   Lockerdown.com

In the US., truck guns are great if you can keep from getting them stolen.

Lost and Found

Prevent Yourself From Becoming Lost

- Every few minutes take a 360° scan to notice the scenery and landmarks.
- Pay special attention to what the scenery looks like behind you. It is what you will see on your way out.
- Be sure the map is large enough to cover the entire area you plan to visit.
- Set your map to a compass. This allows the features on the map and ground to be more easily matched.
- "Blaze" the trail along the way. Save waypoints with GPS. Leave physical markers that can be seen on the return trip.
- If traveling in a convoy, do not continue without seeing the person behind you.

What If You Become Lost

- Retrace the area of travel in your mind and on a map. Do the best you can to remember how you reached the current location.
- Double check the navigation tools available and start backtracking.
- The idea is to get back to a location that you can confirm.
- Carefully reviewing the information will help reduce confusion that can lead to panic.

If still lost, learn to find your way out by doing the following:

- Do not panic, wander around or split up. A superior mental attitude is the greatest factor in a survival situation.

- Make it easy to be found. Think about how you can be seen from the air and the ground. Use whatever materials are available to make a SOS sign. Burn your spare tire to create lots of black smoke. Stay with your vehicle, leave the hood open to indicate something is wrong. The international sign of distress is three markings, fires or sounds.

- Make yourself comfortable. Be optimistic about being found soon while realizing that it may take days.

- Make a plan. It's up to you to assess the situation the best you can, considering all the options available.

- Deadly mistakes: Giving up, splitting up, wandering aimlessly, leaving your vehicle.

Jack's ~~10~~ Twenty Off-Road Essentials

You've heard of the Ten Essentials, that's fine for bare bones backpacking. Off-road outings require a little more gear.

Communications	Drinking Water
Extra Clothing/ Jacket	First Aid & Snake Bite Kit
Flashlights (LED) Batteries	Food (MRE's & Power bars)
Full Sized Spare, High-lift	GPS with Extra Batteries
Knife/Machete	Map and Compass
Matches/Fire Starter	Recovery Gear
Shovel and Axe	Signal Mirror & Whistle
Spare Eyewear	Special Medications
Sunscreen/Sunglasses	Tarp
Toilet Paper	Tool Kit

See a packing lists in **Appendix B**.

 Get a backpack and make a 'Bug Out Bag' out of it by loading it up with essentials. It's a practical addition to your truck and you can take it with you if you venture out on foot.

 Update your first aid kit with a snake bite kit, hemostatic bandages, and a tourniquet. These are proven to save lives.

Put the essentials in a backpack and you have a 'Bug Out Bag.'

 The essentials are critical, for the modern traveler, but modern survival also requires two working credit cards and phone chargers.

First Aid

Keep a good first aid kit in your truck and a smaller kit in your *Bug Out Bag*. Both kits will have to have a little extra than what they provide over the shelf. You will need to clean and close lacerations that will require more than a band aid. Also bring a first aid reference manual that is easy to read. Here is a CPR summary in a paragraph.

If you come across someone who is not breathing and you cannot feel a pulse, they maybe already technically dead. This is the time to start CPR. The recommentiations change over the years, but now on an adult it is 30 chest compressions to two breaths. If they wake up, throw up or yell 'ouch,' stop, you saved their life. If they fail to come back, you did what you could, they had probably already passed before you started.

 If you need to perform CPR, the victim is already dead. Many don't help because they are afraid of getting sued. Most counties including the U.S. has Good Samaritan laws to place to protect you.

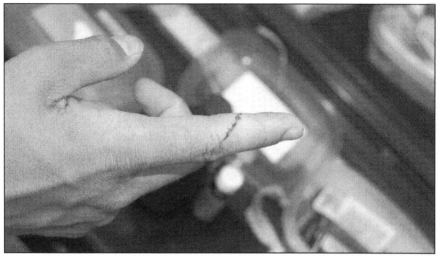

First aid means cleaning and closing lacerations that typically require more than the band aids provided in small over the counter kits. This cut was cleaned with hydrogen peroxide and sealed with super glue.

It seems the most common requirement of first aid is to deal with cuts and lacerations. I carry a bottle of hydrogen peroxide. It is cheaper and easier to get than iodine and it does a great job of cleaning wounds. You may need to apply pressure with a clean dressing first to stop the bleeding. Once cleaned, you will also need to close the wound and dress with direct pressure to keep it from bleeding.

There are several ways to close wounds. Few people want to or know how to apply sutures or stitches. Thankfully, there are other options like butterfly bandages and super glue. Larger lacerations could be closed with safety pins and even duct tape before the patient can get to a doctor.

Deep cuts and bullet wounds can be treated with self-clotting hemostatic bandages. These bandages save lives by helping the blood coagulate to stop the bleeding. In extreme cases, a tourniquet is used on arms and legs. Write down the time it was applied on the patient, this could help the doctors save the limb.

First Aid Kit Extras

Besides all the bandages and band aids that come in an over-the-counter kit, make sure you also have the following:

Items to Close Wounds Butterfly Bandages, Super Glue, Safety Pins, Duct Tape, and a Suture Stitches Kit if you know how to use it.

Medications Extra Strength Pain Killer, Antibiotic Ointment, Benadryl Cream and Pills, Anti-Diarrhea Pills, Eye Drops and Hydrogen Peroxide. Bonus; Sunblock and Insect Repellant

Other Items Snake Bite Kit, Hemostatic Combat Bandages, Tourniquet, Scalpel, Tweezers, Needle, Feminine Hygiene Products.

The Least You Need to Know

- You can't plan for every scenario so plan ahead the best you can and surround yourself with smart people who know how to solve problems.

- Survival is a mental game inspired by a self-fulfilling prophecy meaning you can or cannot do what you believe you can.

- Whatever you think you need to survive, there are people around the world operating on much less.

- Be a traveler not a tourist. Invest the time to learn as much as possible about the area.

- Telling someone where you are going gives you a fighting chance of someone looking for you if you fail to return.

- Do not travel through unknown territory without the ability to communicate and navigate.

- The best food and water are what you bring with you.

- If you must defend yourself against dangerous animals or people, your vehicle should include a number of items to do so such as: machete, axe, shovel and tire iron.

- One of the best ways not to get lost is to continue to look behind you for a 'reverse prospective.' This allows you to see what it should look like on your return trip back.

- Understand how to use your GPS's track log to backtrack on an electronic breadcrumb trail to find your way back.

- Get a backpack and make your own 'Bug Out Bag,' with all the necessary items and essentials you need.

- Update your first aid kit with a snake bite kit, hemostatic bandages, and a tourniquet.

18. OFF ROAD REPAIRS

Off-Road 911, Fixing Stuff on the Trail.

Unless you are an off-road racer with a semi-truck support team budget, you are limited with space like the rest of us. That typically means one tool bag and another box or bag full of duct tape, zip ties, jumper cables and other spare parts. That is really going to limit what kind of repairs we can make on the trail. Ideally, when traveling in a group, each person brings their own variety of tools and parts. This works out great because within the group's supply, someone has the right part, tools, and skill to get you up and rolling again.

When thinking about on-the trail-breakdowns, we can classify most problems into four categories: First, completely unexpected major mechanical breakdowns like blown engines, transmissions, drivetrain, or electric/computer system failures. Not much you can do about these epic failures on the trail. Sometimes the best you can hope for is to tow strap the truck back to the pavement and wait for a tow truck.

The second category is breakdowns due to lack of maintenance. Basic tune-up parts such as belts, hoses, old fluids, corroded battery cables that are neglected and not replaced until they fail. A truth of off-road travel is that if you fail to maintain your truck, the weak link will reveal itself on the trail. Why? All the bumping, shaking and vibration stresses parts and systems far beyond any typical street driving.

Blown radiator hose on the trail. Too strange of shape to repair with a generic hose, so rush-ordered one. This expense could have possibly been prevented if replaced while doing regular maintenance.

The third category is driver error. It is the nut behind the wheel that pushes the truck beyond its limits. The operator overdrives for speed and performance until they crash and/or stress parts until they break. Maybe you can fix these problems on the trail, or not. But either way, it's an expensive and stupid mistake to make by not driving to the practical capability of the driver's experience and the limits of the vehicle.

Fuel filters are often neglected and eventually they can become clogged, cutting off the fuel supply to the engine. Replace them every two years and write the date on the filter as a reminder.

The fourth category falls under somewhat normal off-road wear and tear. Even if driving within your experience and vehicle's capacity, Murphy's Law still applies, meaning you will break things.

 Any weak link or un-maintained part of your truck will only be multiplied once you are off-road. It is easier and cheaper to repair and replace parts in a garage then on the trail.

For example, after a recent desert run with much sand, mud and water, my engine starting choking and running rough triggering my 'Check Engine Light.' I did a walk around, under hood and under engine inspection and found a disconnected vacuum line. Plugging in the vacuum line helped smooth out the engine but it was obvious something else was still wrong. The next step was to scan the system for codes that triggered the Check Engine Light. A code scanner picked up two: P0171 Engine too lean, and P0303 Misfire in cylinder 3.

The disconnected vacuum line explains the first code from the intake system sucking extra air in from an open line.

A cylinder misfire is often from a bad spark plug or coil pack. I thought this was strange because in the attempt to follow my own advice, I recently replaced both the plugs and coils. I pulled the plug and it looked ok, but after inspecting the coil, the inside spring that contacts the top of the plug was corroded. It looked as if water leaked into the spark plug port. After a good cleaning and a heavy shot of *WD-40*, it was all put back together again.

Before starting the engine, I disconnected the negative battery cable for one minute to clear the two system codes. After a test drive I was relieved that the engine ran great and no more error codes came back on. In this case, two problems were easily fixed without spending money.

Your vehicle will get scrapes and dents and depending on your personality, this could be a serious ego blow. Or, you could wear the battle damage like a badge of honor. Either way, body and paint damage will not stop you. Following, is a list of common breakdown problems that are commonly experienced on the trail.

See a list of suggested tools in **Appendix B**. At the very minimum, carry enough tools and know how to do the following:

Change a Tire
Skill Level: Basic
Tools: High-lift jack, lug wrench or ½" drive ratchet with impact socket, wheel chocks (could be rocks or wood chunks).

SAR specialist John Miller changes a flat on his tidy Defender 90.

This should be the first thing any driver learns to do, driving off-road or not. As soon as you notice a flat tire, drive to flat ground.
Never attempt to change a tire on at an incline or off-camber slope.

Put the vehicle in Park or in gear, set the brake, and chock two of the other tires to prevent the vehicle from rolling. Break lose the lug nuts on the flat tire wheel. Then jack up the vehicle until the flat tire is off the ground. If your tires are larger than 33", you will most likely need a high-lift style jack, as your factory scissor jack will probably not be tall or secure enough to work safely.

Finish unbolting the lug nuts until the flat tire can be pulled off. Replace with a full-sized spare and carefully tighten the lugs by hand first to keep them from cross-threading. Carefully tighten them further with the socket, then lower the jack until the new tire is on the ground. Now tighten each lug tight in a cross-star manner where once one is tight, you move to the opposite lug across the wheel from the other. Repeat until all lugs are tight. Check the lugs again once you hit pavement.

Jump Start, Check or Replace a Dead Battery
Skill Level: Basic
Tools: Jumper cables, small wrench or socket, voltmeter.

Battery problems can be common off-road for two reasons. One is all the accessories like axillary lights, winch, and an electric refrigerator all causes extra stress on the battery, especially if you are running just one. The second is the vibration. The internal workings can literally shake apart.

If your battery is dead or engine turning over slowly, it could be low or damaged.

 Never venture off-road with corroded or damaged battery terminal clamps or cables. This type of simple maintenance needs to be done in your driveway and not on the trail.

Using a voltmeter, you can take a quick reading by putting the leads on the positive and negative terminals. A healthy battery should read 12 to just over 13 volts. Check the terminals. If you can wiggle them loose or they are covered in white powder corrosion, you will need to take them apart, clean and tighten them back up. Use a wire brush, terminal cleaner kit or sandpaper. It does not hurt to coat them with a spray cleaner like WD-40. If you are replacing the battery or cleaning the terminals, remove the ground (black or – marked) cable first.

If you need to jump a dead battery, use two people to carefully attach the jumper cable clamps to each battery, red on red and black and black. Do not let the cable ends touch each other or any other metal to prevent them from shorting out. Let the vehicle doing the jumping mid-rev idle for a minute or two before turning over the dead vehicle. It could start right up. If nothing happens or the starter just clicks, give it a little more time. Once the dead vehicle starts, carefully remove the jumper cable clamps from each battery and let the engine run long enough to charge the low battery.

Indian Special Forces, near Nahan, India
Trucks with manual transmissions can be push started by popping the transmission in first or second gear once it gets rolling.

Broken Driveshaft U-Joint or Axle Components
Skill Level: Basic
Tools: Two small wrenches.

Another common problem is broken driveshaft u-joints. The u-joint is the flexible knuckle on each end of the driveshaft. These knuckles have grease zerks in them that often get overlooked causing the u-joint to go dry of lube and eventually break apart.

In a 2WD vehicle, you are not driving out without replacing the drive shaft or broken u-joint. In a 4WD, you have another option. Simply unbolt the broken driveshaft and remove it, then place the transfer case into 4WD. For example, if your rear driveshaft is broken, you can drive out with your front axle.

This also applies if your driveshafts are OK, but you break hubs, axles or ring and pinion gears. For example, locked differentials can easily break axles or other components. If necessary, remove the driveshaft to the broken axle, place the transfer case in 4WD and drive out on the good axle.

 Carry a code scanner. Once used only by mechanics, these scanners are now available for under $60 and easily plug in to a port under the dash. Repairs are much easier and less expensive to fix by seeing what error code had been tripped.

Electrical Problems
Skill Level: Basic to Advanced
Tools: Multimeter, spare wire, spare fuses, tape, zip ties.

The vibration from off-road driving can shake to death electronic components as well as wear wire coatings down to a bare metal to short out. If an electrical system stops working, the easy thing to check is the fuse box, then check your owner's manual to locate the fuse of the system not working. Bring a coil of wire to bypass fuses and relays when needing to hard wire or test parts.

Changing a blown fuse may fix the problem, but often only temporarily because something has caused the fuse to blow in the first place. Check the wiring and components carefully for signs of wires unplugged or wearing. Also, look for any indication of burning or discoloration from excessive heat or water damage.

Some critical electrical components include: the CPU computer module, fuel pump and electric fan motor. Highly modified vehicles, like off-road race cars have redundant systems. They carry two CPU's, have two fuel pumps with an A-B toggle switch easily allowing the driving to change pumps. Also, a manual override switch to turn on electric fans in the event the electric thermostat fails.

 Electronic CPR? Electric components like fuel pumps and starter solenoids can sometimes be bumped back to life with a blow from a hammer. It will not repair the problem, but it might get you home!

Engine Will Not Start
Skill Level: Intermediate to Advanced
Tools: Basic tools to engine diagnostic scanner.

If the starter motor turns and the engine will still not start, there is probably a fuel supply or spark problem.

In the old carburetor days, this was easier to do. You could take off the air filter and physically look down the throat of the carburetor, working the throttle linkage and see gas spraying through the jets. It's a little more complicated with fuel injection. Remove the filter and shoot some starter fluid or *WD-40* and you should hear the engine try to start or pop. If the engine is starving for fuel, it could be a clogged fuel filter or a failed fuel pump.

If it is not a fuel issue, it could be lack of spark. This is easy to check by placing a screwdriver into the end of a spark plug wire and setting the screwdriver on the engine, so the shaft of the screwdriver is approximately ¾" away from a metal bracket. Turning over the engine, you would see a spark jump from the screwdriver to the metal bracket. If you don't have spark plug wires, you can do the same thing with a coil pack.

If no spark, there is the problem. On older systems, check the distributor, cap and rotor. There could be cracks in the plastic or a buildup of moisture. Ignition points could also be burnt or damaged. Modern computer-controlled systems are more difficult to diagnose. Wiring harness moving from the CPU computer to ignition modular(s) to coil packs. Check fuses and relays relating to the ignition system. If exposed to water and mud, the connectors can be unplugged to be checked and cleaned with *WD-40*. If still no luck, it may be a matter of testing and replacing electronic components.

Leaking Fluids

Skill Level: Basic
Tools: Basic tools, duct tape, hose clamps, stop-leak glue and fluids.

Replace your spring clamps with real hose clamps before off-roading.

One of the primary sources of leaking fluids is from the radiator and cooling system. Hoses get neglected, dry rot, crack and leak. Maintenance is critical as hoses are much easier and cheaper to fix in a shop than out on the trail.

Weston Miller

Replace your hoses before you need to and save the old ones for spares. Also, replace the factory spring clamps with real hose clamps. Split, leaking hoses can be patched a couple of ways. One way is to dry off the hose, fill the crack with glue or silicone sealant, then tape up the outside with duct tape, then place hose clamps down on the tape. This might get you back to civilization. A better option if possible is to cut the hose on the split and sleeve the inside with a metal or plastic pipe or tube, then glue and tighten down with hose clamps.

Radiator cooling tubes, water pumps and expansion tanks also leak. Sometimes you can glue cracks up if they can be exposed, cleaned and dried with products like *JB Weld*. Other products like *Stop-Leak* are poured into the radiator once cooled, and the product finds and seals leaks from the inside out.

When engine and fluid pans are punctured, they can sometimes be patched with two-part mixable puttles or glue like *JB Weld*. There are also liquid stop-leak products for engine, transmission and gear boxes that are a good idea to take along.

Radiator Thermostat Stuck Open or Closed
Skill Level: None
Tools: Your vehicle's heater

If your thermostat is stuck open, your radiator will be circulating coolant constantly causing longer for your engine to reach an operating temperature.

Turning the heater off will help the engine warm up faster. If your truck's thermostat is stuck closed, your radiator shuts off causing the engine to overheat. When shut, engine coolant circulates through the engine block only, but this includes the heater core.

Turning on your heater full blast will help cool the engine. Not fun when it is already hot outside, but it could save your engine from damage while you are trying to get back to civilization.

Recovery From Tip Over
Skill Level: Intermediate
Tools: Basic, recovery gear, fire extinguishers, first aid

If a vehicle has tipped over or completely rolled over, it is time to take immediate action. First, shut off the ignition and look for leaking fuel. Ideally the occupants were seatbelted in and can safely exit as soon as possible. If they are unable, you will have to help them while taking extreme caution of moving anyone who could have neck or back injuries.

Trail Nomads

After a rollover it's time to take action. Shutting off the ignition, checking for leaking fuel and triaging the passengers.

If there is no spilt fuel or smoke, you could leave them in place for paramedics, but they may need to be removed anyway to perform other first aid care such as bleeding wound care or even CPR. Ultimately, you will have to make the call based upon an assesment of injuries and immediate danger like an unstable vehicle that could burst into flames or continue to roll over.

If the vehicle can be pulled back up on its wheels, it may be drivable. Carefully check for leaks and damage. Check to see if the tires are good and the wheels or axles are not bent. If it looks operable, turn over the ignition. If the engine turns, but will not start, it could be a collision sensor has shut off the fuel pump. If so, find and press the inertia button that acts as a circuit breaker switch to restart the fuel pump.

 After every off-road trip, do a walk around of your vehicle to check for damage, low tires and if there is any leaking of fluids. Don't neglect to look underneath the undercarriage as well.

Undercarriage Damage
Skill Level: Basic
Tools: Tarp or roller to lay on, flashlight.

Bang around on the rocks and sooner or later there is going to be damage in the undercarriage. We are used to looking for scratches and dents on the top side but should not forget to inspect underneath the truck when we do our walk around.

Common damage areas include tie rods and other steering components. If you take a hard hit to the front end and your steering wheel is no longer in alignment, that is a big indication that you have steering system damage. Your front end will be out of alignment, but depending on the level of damage, you would still be able to get back to civilization. Back in the shop, your tie rods will have to be straightened or replaced, possibly even sleeved with steel tubing to make them stronger. Then a front-end inspection and alignment to ensure you are back on track.

After every off-road excursion, make a habit out of walking around and inspecting your undercarriage carefully looking for leaks and damage. Check brake lines, parking brake lines, fuel line, wire looms, skid plates, leaking oil pans from the differentials, transfer case, engine and transmission. Other problem areas can include bent or damaged exhaust pipes or mufflers as well as leaking fuel tanks.

Water in Air Intake
Skill Level: Intermediate
Tools: Spark plug socket and ratchet, breaker bar and socket to turn crank shaft.

If you drive through deep water and believe you may have sucked some into your engine, shut off the motor immediately.

A snorkel will not completely protect your engine from water damage. The airbox and intake system must be carefully sealed as well as the electrical systems and vent tubes will be needed from all the differentials and any other gear boxes where water can enter.

Even if in the middle of a river crossing, your engine cannot take water in the cylinders. The water's hydraulic pressure will destroy the motor.

Get a recovery tow to dry land to assess the damage. If your fuel tank, oil tanks and electrical system is not full of water, you might be in luck. Pull all the spark plugs and carefully turn over the engine to cycle any water in the cylinders that may have been sucked in.

Taking the plugs out eliminates the pressure allowing the water to cycle through without further damage to the engine heads and block. Replace the spark plugs and check your fluid levels. Checking your ignition components to dry them and spray with *WD-40* is a good idea. Give it a turn and see if the engine will fire.

The Least You Need to Know

- Off-road mechanical problems typically fall into four categories; 1. Major and unexpected. 2. From lack of maintenance. 3. Over-driving vehicle. 4. Normal wear and tear.

- Any weak link or un-maintained part of your truck will only be multiplied once off-road.

- It is cheaper and easier to fix maintenance problems in the shop instead of on the trail.

- After realizing you have a flat tire, do not stop until you are on stable flat ground.

- Never venture off-road with damaged or corroded battery clamps or cables.

- Carrying a code scanner is an excellent idea and can make troubleshooting repairs much easier and less expensive.

- You may be able to still drive back with drivetrain damage by disconnecting the drive shaft to the damaged axle.

- If traveling to remote areas, consider carrying a spare fuel pump, fuel filter, CPU computer and ignition module.

- If an engine turns over but does not start, it is typically a lack of fuel or spark issue.

- Replace hoses and belts before you need them and save them as spares.

- There are several stop-leak products for cooling systems to oil pans that make sense to carry along.

- A snorkel alone will not protect your vehicle from deep water crossings. The electrical systems and every fluid tank needs to be sealed and vented to a height equal to the snorkel intake.

19. EXPEDITION VEHICLES AND TRAILERS

Home on the Range

The fun of overlanding is setting up a home away from home you can take with you about anywhere. If you are traveling with a full-sized truck, you can always crash in the back and call it good. But, most of us drive smaller rigs and need more room to be comfortable. Luckily there are lots of options of what you can buy and make, as well as many budget options from 'garage sale cheap' to 'the sky is the limit.'

Regardless of your style of off-road camping, there are some key elements to consider. Your gear needs to be durable, lightweight, functional and waterproof. Every time you camp, it gives you the opportunity to adjust what to bring and to determine what gear works best for your preferred use.

Overland Camping Formats

We will look at the pros, cons and expense of the various camping formats that include the following:

Ground Tents	Roof Top Tents (RTTs)
Off-Road Trailers	Pickup Campers
Off-Road Vans	Expedition RVs and Motorhomes

Kez Danielle

*Setting up your expedition camp gear is as much fun as using it.
Kez sets up her new RTT before her next adventure.*

Ground Tents

Don't laugh, your parents probably took you camping this way and you survived just fine. You probably even had fun. Yes, you can wake up in a pool of water if its raining, but this method of camping is tried and true for thousands of years. Ground tents come in a enough shapes and sizes to fit about every application and an expedition quality tent is still less than a third of the price of a RTT (Roof Top Tent).

It is a good idea to bring a couple of tarps, one as ground cover to set the tent up on, the second to place over the top as an added rain fly. Regarless of the camping format you use, it's a good idea to bring along a ground tent to set up as a spare room. Great for drop in camping guests, kids or storing gear out of the weather.

Price: $40-$400.

Pro: Low cost and reliable, easy to pack and use. Possibly safer than climbing up and down from the rooftops.

Con: A little longer to set up than an RTT. Also being on the ground, more exposed to water, mud and things that creep in the night.

Application: Ideal for campers on a budget. It is also good to carry one along as a spare room for guests or gear.

North Face Talus 4 is a good example of an expedition quality four person rated tent (more like for two with gear), for around $300.

 Regardless of what type of camping you do, it's a good idea to bring along a ground tent to use as a guest room or store gear.

Roof Top Tents, RTTs

Inspired by African safaris, RTTs have exploded in popularity over the last 20 years and have become mainstream. There's just something off-the-dial cool about having a tent on your roof.

Where you park is where you camp. They also deploy fast by pulling down a ladder and folding the top up.

Most also have a built in or contained mattress, so making your bed is as simple as throwing up sleeping bags and you are good to crash. The roofrack needed for the RTT is also an excellent platform for an awning.

Brett Clifaldi

There is something epic about having your camp on your roof.

There are a few things things to consider before lightening your wallet by $1,200 and adding 100 pounds to your roof. There is a cost for coolness and the extra weight on the roof rack does make your vehicle a little top heavy. Roof racks and RTTs also mess up your already brick-like aerial dynamics, possibly costing you a MPG. Taking a leak in the middle of the night can also become a chore. Negotiating a ladder half-asleep is not fun or safe. Consider a plastic bottle with a widemouth lid for a chamber-pot.

Another issue with roof top camping is that it is great to be self-contained, but once you are set up, you are stuck. Meaning you cannot just drive off to make a B-double E, double-R U N.

 With a RTT it's a good idea to use a container with a closable lid to pee in to avoid going up and down a ladder in the middle of the night.

Price: $900-$2500 for folding tent, $3,000 + for hard shell.

Pro: Self-contained camping, where your home is ready anywhere, anytime and in minutes. No messing with tents on a muddy ground or a trailer to tow.

Con: RTTs with roof racks make your truck top heavy. Expensive and taking a midnight leak can be challenging.

Application: Ideal for frequent campers who want their tent already packed and deployable at a moment's notice.

Pacific Coast Rover Club

Inspired by African safaris, RTTs have become mainstream.

Jimmy Crawford

Zip on lower rooms provide much needed extra space to make RTTs more livable. These are ideal for gear storage, dressing and getting out of the weather.

Off-Road Trailers

Trailers are the ultimate accessory for a truck and a great way to store all of your camp gear in one place to have it ready to go. Including a tent, a kichen, coolers, bedding, propane and fuel. Because they are dedicated to your next adventure, you can continue to update your packing list, giving you a little more peace of mind, knowing you have more room for all those things you might need. With a place for gear storage, trailers also take the weight off your vehicle for daily driving.

One of the main advantages of using a trailer is that once you set up your camp, you can un-hook. Now your vehicle is free and ready to play without all that extra weight and gear. Then upon your return, your basecamp is all set up and waiting for you to enjoy. There is a price to all this convenience, about 2-3,000 pounds of metal to tow behind your truck. Towing off-road, even a light trailer can be fun, but it is also a bit of pain. One of the main problems is that you can get down a narrow trail with no place to turn around. From off-road to driving through a gas station, pulling a trailer means planning your route ahead of time.

I was once pulling an off-road trailer down a narrow trail at night in a rainstorm. I soon realized that there was no good place to turn around and visibility was terrible. I attempted a multi-point turn around and, in the mud, and rain, the trailer slid off the trail placing a tree between the back of the truck and the front of the trailer. I had to disconnect the trailer, pull the front over with a tow strap and hook it back out again. By the time I got out, I had badly bent my front trailer tongue jack and managed to jack-knife the trailer into my rear quarter panel, but at that point, I was just happy to see pavement.

Adam Tolman's Toyota Land Cruiser and trailer.
Moab is not a terrible place to wake up in the morning.

Whether you build a trailer or buy one, consider using a military pintle-style hitch. The truck's receiver clamps down through the trailer's donut so it will not bounce apart on the trail. Pintle hitches are clunky, but I would not use a ball hitch off-road. If you can drive through it, the pintle mounted trailer will still be behind you.

Price: $3,000 to $40,000.

Pro: The ultimate accessory to your truck, paint to match with the same wheels and even better. A great way to shed weight off your truck by having all your camp gear already attached to or inside the trailer.

Con: Trailers can be a pain to pull off-road. Before you pull into a narrow alley or trail, make sure there is room to drive through or turn around to get back out.

Application: Ideal for campers who want a full basecamp, but not bog down their own truck with all the extra weight and gear. Perfect for drivers who want to play with their trucks once camp has been set up.

Benjamin Weight's pod trailer with matching JK is ideal for carrying camping gear and just big enough to use as a bedroom.

 When pulling a trailer, remember not to go down a trail that does not go through or you cannot turn around.

David Rod's Vector is a great example of a trailer small enough to be pulled anywhere behind a Jeep with lots of locking storage boxes and a roof rack for a roof top tent and awning.

The Vector has a very tidy pop out kitchen with sink, stove and a slide-out countertop cook space.

The benefit of pulling a trailer around is that you have needed room for creature comforts like a hot water heater for showers, water tanks, propane, solar powered 12v systems and electric refrigerators.

 One of the advantages of a trailer is the ability to pack extra gear like kitchen supplies, food and bedding without bogging down your truck.

The fun of off-road trailers is making your own. Using military trailers can be a lower cost option like Lindi Jensen's M416 conversion.

Military trailers are a great way to build on a budget. The primary modification needed is wiring and LED lights that are inexpensive and something you can probably do yourself. Hub adapters are also available to match your truck's wheel bolt pattern.

I built this trailer to haul explosives to work at remote mine locations. M116 military flatbed with an 8' Royal service box welded on top. Then topped off with a Canadian Box Tent.

Once the Box Tent is cranked up and popped out it provides two twin or one king sized bed with an awning off the back.

Inside the Box Tent is quite roomy and the fiberglass top provides a little more shelter in weather. They were only imported in the U.S. for a year or two and hard to find.

Off-Road Vans

I am old enough to remember the van craze of the late 70's and early 80's. Vans were bought up to be converted into cool luxury cruisers with captains chairs, beds, plush upholstery and kitchenettes. High gas prices were most likely to blame for wiping that fad out, but there has always been an allure to owning and driving a custom van. There has always been RV camper-style vans availible, but even better if they have 4WD with off-road capability.

Van manufactures have not done a good job of releasing 4WD vans so companies like *SportsMobile* and *UJoint* have been converting vans to 4WD for years. They can take a factory 2WD van and replace the front suspension with a solid axle, adding a transfer case and driveshaft for four-wheel drive. Converting a stock van into a 4WD home-away-from home is not cheap, but if you like to get off the beaten path, there is nothing else like it.

Vans provide a sense of convience, privacy and security no other vehicle can. First of all, vans are not so big that you can't drive them off-road. Your favorite beach, desert or snow-covered mountain road, no problem.

Second, you can stop pretty much anywhere you want and sleep. No one is probably going to bother you because they cannot see you. Third, you are also in a weatherproof metal shell with lockable doors and windows instead of behind tent fabric so there is something to appreciate about that increased level of security.

Pam Beckman

From cross-country road trips to exploring the Baja Peninsula, if you need a van you need a van, but it is going to cost you. Most likely from lower production numbers, vans are considerably more expensive than similarly-equipped trucks and SUVs. A nicely equipped 4x4 van with some basic off-road accessories, $70,000 easy. Build one or buy one, either way, it's easy to enjoy the ultimate off-road camping escape pod.

Sportsmobile

Mercedes offers a turbo diesel option that provides decent mileage, like 14-18 MPG for their 188-hp 3.0-liter V6 BlueTec engine.

Price:	$35,000 to $90,000+.

Pro: Mild trail off-road capable, convenient, sleep anywhere with some level of privacy in a secure, self-contained platform.

Con: Higher ticket purchase price. Full-size vans have poor gas mileage, mid-size diesel vans have more reasonable gas mileage. Ideal for no more than two people as the interior can become cramped quickly.

Application: Ideal for campers who do frequent or long-distance trips, who want the flexibility to sleep or camp wherever they want.

Pickup Campers

Pickup campers have been around as long as pickups, but the off-road variety are typically ruggedized, lighter weight and designed with pop up tops. These are made by companies like: *Four Wheel, Northstar, Palamino* and *Alaskan*.

There are a number of advantages of using these campers. One is you can use the pickup you already have. If no truck yet and on a budget, you can easily pick up a late model gas or diesel pickup that will easily carry one at a fraction of the price of a newer truck. These come in all sizes so they can be used on a mid-size to one-ton plus pickup. Campers can also be used on a flatbed. Some are made just for a flatbed application. Some place a regular camper on a flatbed and run aluminum storage boxes down each side to fill in the space.

Chris Tillaart is still overlanding in the original
Turtle III with a Four Wheel brand pop up camper.

The pop up variety are also reasonably lightweight, approximately 700 to 1100 pounds based upon size and options. Having the top crank down reduces drag and helps maintain a lower center of gravity for off-road driving. Gas trucks will see a decrease in mileage, a diesel truck will hardly know its even there. With jackable legs, they are also easy to remove when not needed on the back of your truck. Having a camper also leaves your rear bumper open for towing a boat or another trailer.

Price: $9,000-$19,000.

Pro: Use the pickup you already have or buy a late-model one if on a budget. Self-contained but still lightweight and low profile for off-road driving. Easy to remove from pickup bed when not in use.

Con: Limited in space but beats a tent.

Application: Ideal for campers who already have a pickup they want to use or on a budget to pick up an older diesel truck.

Erik Claus

Pop up off-road campers are ideal for those who are on a budget to use later-model diesel pickups. The weight of the camper is negotiable compared to using them on ¾ ton gas pickups.

Another advantage with pop up campers is they are lighter weight and provide a lower center of gravity while driving.

 One of the major advantages of campers is that you can use the truck you already have, they don't limit off-road capability, easy to remove when not in use and your hitch is still availible to tow something else.

Expedition Motorhomes and RVs

Need a motorhome-sized vehicle with 4WD and off-road capability? It is possible, but not cheap. Whether you make your own or purchase something already build, this full-sized convenience comes with a real estate-sized price tag. Obviously these big off-road rigs are not for everyone, but if you are going full-time and not be limited where you drive, they may just be for you.

There certainly is something unique about being to travel about anywhere you want in the world, back roads and off the grid with a level of comfort when you get there. Like having water, electricity, a kitchen, a real bed, a shower and a toilet. It takes the work out of camping which is ideal for full-timers or extended trips.

There are a few companies that make full sized expedition vehicles making it possible to get a rig turn-key ready to go from the solar panels to the water filteration system. But if on a budget and you would like to build your own, there are other options possibly at a fraction of the cost.

Park Ranger, Meg Chamberlain makes an motorhome from a 2006 Ford E450 Superduty ambulance. Original purchase price $8,500.

One option is to look at an ambulance platform. Good diesel ambulances are sold, some with 4WD for sometimes much less than a pickup with the same motor. They are a good balance in size providing enough room for a kitchen and a bed, but still small enough to take off-road. They are typically diesel and the rear boxes are well built out of aluminum with plently of storage cabinets inside and out.

Another option is a military transport truck like the *Stewart & Stevenson M1079*. These 4WD trucks are battlefield-proven and come with a *Cat* straight six cylinder diesel engine. They are sold at government and other vehicle auctions with low miles at a fraction of their original cost.

Building a full-sized expedition truck is not a simple or a low-cost endeavor. The best couple to get advice from is Gary and Monika Wescott. The Westcott's have been building expedition vehicles and traveling the world since 1972. Their self-contained expedition vehicles like the *Turtle V* was partially inspired by not having the inconvenience of pulling an off-road trailer.

From the Wescott's: "Don't buy a new truck. Look around and find an old one, specifically one that will run on any kind of diesel anywhere in the world and carry the load you are anticipating. I can certainly personally recommend the *Ford F550* with its 17,500-pound weight capacity or the even the *Dodge 5500* which is a comparable vehicle. You need to pick an engine that can be worked on in foreign countries and one that will run on regular road diesel, any kind that comes out of the pump. A manual transmission is by far the best choice!

First you need to decide where you're going and for how long. Will you be visiting National Parks, taking weekend trips to the beaches of Mexico, or driving around the world? If the former, do you really need four-wheel drive, a winch, and locking differentials? Is it going to be warm and sunny where you're going? Your personal level of comfort is critical. Can you really stand sleeping in a rooftop tent for two weeks in 85°F and pounding rain in the middle of Brazil?

The second consideration is who you are traveling with. Will it be just yourself and a companion, or with two kids, a cat and a dog? These factors will influence both camper size and equipment needed. Once again, where are you going, with who, and how comfortable do you want to be? The catch is, if you go too big or too heavy, or you are overloaded, you won't be able to get to the places you wanted to go.

The advantage of owning an American pickup truck is that there are millions of them out there with thousands of companies making products just a little better and a little stronger than what Detroit could afford to use on an assembly line vehicle. Better bearings, better brakes, better water pumps, better air filters, better turbos, better U-joints, you name it. Some company is making something better to replace something that might break on the road of adventure when you are thousands of miles from home or the nearest dealership. Take the money you save from buying a new vehicle and use it for aftermarket parts to make your truck better and stronger.

The *Tortuga Expedition Camper* was designed and built by us. We saw what the Europeans were using for their expedition vehicles and gained from many of their ideas. Our goal was to build a camper as big on the inside and as small on the outside as possible. After some 35 years of traveling back roads around the world we pretty much knew where we wanted to go and what kind of a vehicle could go there. The camper was built to be comfortable for two people instead of being uncomfortable for four.

In the construction of the box, we created an exoskeleton of welded aluminum and then fitted panels of fiberglass-covered Nida Core into that frame. They were attached with Sika Flex marine adhesive. After that, it was just a matter of fitting the components, mostly using a tape measure and paper & pencil, to see whether the refrigerator, the water tank, the batteries, the bed, the sink, and all the other components would fit.

One of the most critical elements of the design was the mounting system of the camper on the frame of the *Ford F550*. You cannot twist a box. It will break. Most American and European expedition campers use some kind of a three-point mounting system. We designed our own with the help of the engineers at *Midwest Four-Wheel-Drive*, and it has proven reliable.

When we returned from our Trans-Siberian expedition across all of Siberia in the wintertime, with temperatures below -86°F, and later traveling around parts of Europe, we attended African Safari events and other overland vehicle exhibitions. We saw many ideas that we could incorporated into our *Tortuga Expedition Camper*. We also learned more by visiting factories in Germany *like Unicat, Alu Star* and *Langer & Bock*. Those companies have been designing and building expedition campers for decades.

There were important concepts like using every single square centimeter. Cupboards and shelves were built to fit exactly what we knew what was going to be stored in them. In order to make the camper as big on the inside as possible, our bed collapses into a single couch during the day and folds out into a full bed at night with the fitted sheets already on it. This greatly increases the living space.

Perhaps one of the most interesting ideas the Germans came up with was, where do you put a bathroom and a shower in a small camper? We specifically did not want the classic American-style shit-shower-shave-cook-breakfast-all-at-the-same-time-please-don't-get-the-toilet-paper-wet camper. Angling the sides of the roof was a Russian idea. It gives better clearance, and after all, you don't stand up next to the wall. Eliminating a bed over the cab made it look less like a motorhome and the outside roof rack is extremely useful for carrying extra Jerry cans, firewood and a storage box for travel equipment.

Do you really need that little sink with a special room to brush your teeth when you can reach the kitchen sink without moving your feet, or can you just brush your teeth in the kitchen? The Germans with their Spartan ideas figured this out. Put the shower in the doorway and a *Porta Potti,* that slides out on tracks into the doorway.

Gary and Monika Wescott of Turtle Expedition.com have been building vehicles and traveling the world since 1972.

Don't forget to include a bathing option: A solar bag on the roof, sponge baths, a dive in the ocean with sea-soap or *Joy* detergent, or a real hot shower inside or outside your camper. Be aware that you need to plan on how you will handle personal hygiene before you stink.

Hot water is a real luxury, as we discovered two items that make hot water practical. The *Eberspaecher D5* hydronic is a coolant heater. It is connected to the cooling system of the engine. It has its own little pump that burns fuel from the main diesel tank and heats water 160°F. Depending on where you set the valves, its little internal pump will transfer that hot coolant to whatever you want to heat, including the camper, the engine or, have it pump that hot coolant through a Flat Plate Heat Exchanger and you can have hot running water in the kitchen, in the shower and even the outside shower in three minutes.

A temperature control device keeps the water temperature down to about 120°F so you don't burn yourself. And speaking of heat, the compact diesel-powered *Eberspaecher Airtronic* is our primary heat source in the camper. In addition, while we're driving in cold weather, the hot coolant from the engine is also circulated through a small radiator in the camper to keep things toasty on the road.

Regarding our electrical system, again, taking some ideas from the Germans, we use four deep cycle Odyssey batteries and two more of the same exact batteries in the engine compartment. We ordered the truck with the dual alternator system or the ambulance package as it is called.

The primary 135-amp alternator charges the truck engine batteries for starting. The second alternator, modified to 200 amps, charges through a remote *Balmar* regulator and keeps the batteries in the camper charged.

We also have two BP 85 solar panels to keep the batteries topped off. The reason we have the same common size group 34 *Odyssey* batteries in the camper and the engine is first, *Odyssey* only makes one battery that does everything, deep cycle, marine and starting. Secondly, if one of the engine batteries should die, we can just take one out of the camper and pop it in." Thank you, Gary and Monika, great ideas to consider for making the ultimate expedition vehicle!

Price: $25,000-$400,000+.

Pro: Off-road capable, especially on more open desert roads, while still providing RV creature comforts.

Con: Expensive, large and heavy.

Application: Ideal for those who go full time or do extended trips who want all the extra comfort and room without being limited on what roads they choose to travel.

Seth& Kande Jacobsen of Adventure Driven, created 'Brutus' the ultimate go anywhere RV from a Stewart & Stevenson M1079.

Chris Steuber and the crew at Ujoint Offroad convert vans and RVs to 4WD, this includes Class C style motorhomes.

Examples of companies making 4WD expedition vehicles. Earth Cruiser (left) using a Mitsubishi platform and Earth Roamer (right) using a Ford platform.

The Least You Need to Know

- Camping does not have to be complicated or expensive, there is no shame in using a ground tent.

- Roof top tents and awnings are a great way to be ready for camping anytime by having your home away from home packed on your roof rack.

- An off-road trailer built to match your truck is the ultimate accessory. Probably one of the most practical options for expedition camping, just down pull one down a trail you cannot turn around on.

- Off-road vans are convenient, fun to use, and provide an added level of privacy and security.

- Popup campers are ideal, especially if you already have a pickup to haul it with. They are also light enough not to interfere with your truck's off-road capability.

- Expedition trucks are the ultimate statement in go-anywhere style, survivability and comfort, but they are expensive. The budget-minded can build their own by starting off with a surplus ambulance or military truck.

20. INDEX

Travel Itinerary

Critical information to leave behind at:

[ ] Ranger Station   [ ] Family/friends   [ ] At trailhead

Trip Date: _____ Return Date: _____

Persons:

_____ Cell Phone: _____

_____ Cell Phone: _____

_____ Cell Phone: _____

_____ Cell Phone: _____

Destination: _____

Location Description: _____

Route to Take: _____

_____

Coordinates: _____

Motels/Campgrounds: _____

Alt Communication: Satellite Phone: _____

VHF Radio: _____ CB Channel: _____

Vehicles:

Make: _____ Model: _____ Color: _____ Plate: _____

Make: _____ Model: _____ Color: _____ Plate: _____

_____

_____

_____

Off the Grid, Drive, Navigate & Survive Off-Road

Gear Checklists

Safety & Tire Change

[ ] Full size Spare Tire
[ ] Adequate Jack
[ ] Lug wrench
[ ] Flashlight
[ ] Knife
[ ] Gloves
[ ] Lighter or Matches (waterproof)
[ ] Orange Triangles
[ ] Fire Extinguisher
[ ] Fix a Flat Can
[ ] Extra Ratchet Tiedown Straps
[ ] Shovel
[ ] Rope-Paracord
[ ] Tarp
[ ] Tire Snow Chains
[ ] Sunblock
[ ] Insect Repellent
[ ] Machete
[ ] Axe
[ ] Boots with Socks
[ ] Winter Jacket
[ ] Trash Bags
[ ] _____
[ ] _____
[ ] _____

Tools

[ ] Pliers
[ ] Crescent Wrench
[ ] Hammer
[ ] Screwdrivers
[ ] Vise Grips
[ ] Combination Wrench Set
[ ] 3/8 drive sockets with ratchet
[ ] ½ drive sockets with ratchet
[ ] Multi Meter
[ ] _____
[ ] _____
[ ] _____
[ ] _____

Spare Parts
[ ] Fuses, Assorted
[ ] Bulbs, Assorted
[ ] Hose Clamps, Assorted
[ ] WD-40
[ ] Motor Oil
[ ] Transmission Fluid
[ ] Power Steering Fluid
[ ] Fan Belt
[ ] Distributor Cap & Rotor
[ ] Duct Tape
[ ] Electrical Tape
[ ] Zip Ties
[ ] Bailing Wire
[ ] Electrical Wire
[ ] Nuts, Bolts, Washers
[ ] Radiator Stop Leak
[ ] JB Weld, Super Glue
[ ] _____
[ ] _____
[ ] _____

Recovery Gear
[ ] Recovery strap, 30 feet long, looped ends
[ ] Two 'D' Shackles minimum
If your vehicle is equipped with a Winch:
[ ] Tree Saver Strap, looped ends
[ ] Snatch Block
[ ] Leather Gloves
[ ] _____
[ ] _____
[ ] _____

First Aid
[ ] Band Aids, Assorted
[ ] Hydrogen Peroxide for Cleaning Wounds
[ ] Bandages, Assorted
[ ] Butterfly Bandages, Assorted
[ ] Super Glue for Sealing Wounds
[ ] Tweezers
[ ] Gloves, Sterile Latex
[ ] Israeli Hemostatic Bandages
[ ] Tourniquet

[ ] Bee-Insect Bite Relief
[ ] Pain Killer
[ ] Neosporin Anti-Bacteria Lotion
[ ] Benadryl for Allergic Reactions
[ ] Sutures, Needle and Thread
[ ] _____
[ ] _____
[ ] _____
[ ] _____
[ ] _____

Bugout Backpack

Mid-Size Backpack Filled with the Following:

[ ] Small Flashlight & Headlight
[ ] Survival Knife
[ ] Multi Tool Pliers
[ ] Batteries
[ ] Lighter & Matches (waterproof)
[ ] Compass
[ ] Toilet Paper
[ ] Water Purifier
[ ] Two Bottles of Bottled Water (minimum)
[ ] Two MRE, Meals Ready to Eat
[ ] Candy Bars, Mountain Bars
[ ] Paracord
[ ] Small Tarp
[ ] Garbage Bags, Large
[ ] First Aid Kit, Small
[ ] Gloves
[ ] Hat, Stocking Cap
[ ] Bandana
[ ] Hygiene/Signal Mirror
[ ] Notepad, Small with Pen
[ ] Cell Phone Charger Cable
[ ] _____
[ ] _____
[ ] _____
[ ] _____
[ ] _____
[ ] _____

Appendix C International Contact Information

From the U.S. Government

United States Department of State, Bureau of Consular Affairs
Office of American Citizens Services, Room 4817 N.S.,
2201 'C' St. NW, Washington, DC 20520
(202) 647-5225 or (202) 647-5226

General information page   http://travel.state.gov

Assistance to Americans   http://travel.state.gov/arrest.html
arrested abroad

Doctors & Hospitals Abroad   http://travel.state.gov/acs.html#medical

Embassies & Consulates   http://travel.state.gov/links.html

Embassies with Attorneys
         http://travel.state.gov/judicial_assistance.html#attorneys

Medical Information including   http://travel.state.gov/medical.html
lists of air ambulance and travel insurance companies

Road Safety Abroad   http://travel.state.gov/road_safey.html

Travel Warnings Abroad   http://travel.state.gov/travel_warnings.html

United Kingdom Travel Advisories   www.fco.gov.uk/travel/

Welfare/Whereabouts   http://travel.state.gov/where.html
of Americans Overseas

Contact Information for Mexico

In Case of Emergency: Mexican Ministry of Tourism 24-hour hotline,
telephone (55) 5250-0123, or national toll free (01) 800-903-9200. The
Mexican "911" is 060 in Mexico City, or 066; in the rest of Mexico, 066.

U.S. Embassy in Mexico City
Paseo de la Reforma 305, Colonia Cuauhtemoc, 06500 Mexico, D.F.
Tel.: (+52) 55-5080-2000, Fax: (+52) 55-5080-2005
http://www.usembassy-mexico.gov/emenu.html

U.S. Consulate General in Ciudad Juarez
Paseo de la Victoria #3650, Fracc. Partido Senecú
Ciudad Juárez, Chihuahua, Mexico C.P. 32543
Tel.: 656-227-3000, From the U.S.: 1-844-528-6611

U.S. Consulate General in Guadalajara
Progreso 175, Col. Americana, Codigo Postal 44160
Guadalajara, Jalisco, Mexico
Tel.: (+52) 33-3268-2100, Fax: (+52) 33-3825-1951

U.S. Consulate General in Hermosillo
141 Monterey Street, Col. Esqueda, C.P. 83000
Hermosillo, Sonora, Mexico
Tel.: (+52) 662-690-3262, Fax: (+52) 662-217-2571

U.S. Consulate General in Matamoros
Calle Constitución No. 1, Colonia Jardín,
Matamoros, Tamaulipas 87330
Tel.: (+52) 868-208-2000, Fax: (+52) 868-816-0883

U.S. Consulate General in Merida
Calle 60 No. 338-K x 29 y 31, Col. Alcala Martin Merida,
Yucatan, Mexico 97050
Tel.: (+52) 999-942-5700, Fax: (+52) 999-942-5758

U.S. Consulate General in Monterrey
Prolongación Ave. Alfonso Reyes #150
Col. Valle del Poniente, Santa Catarina, Nuevo León
México 66196
Tel.: (+52) 81-8047-3100, Fax: (+52) 81-8342-5433

U.S. Consulate General in Nogales
Calle San José s/n, Fraccionamiento los Alamos
C. P. 84065 Nogales, Sonora
Tel.: (+52) 631-311-8150, Fax: (+52) 631-313-4652

U.S. Consulate General in Nuevo Laredo
Paseo Colon 1901, Colonia Madero
Nuevo Laredo, Tamaulipas 88260
Tel.: 867 714 0512 (from México), 867-714-0512 (from the US)

U.S. Consulate General in Tijuana
Paseo de las Culturas s/n, Mesa de Otay
Delegación Centenario C.P. 22425, Tijuana, Baja California
Tel.: (664) 977-2000

U.S. Embassies and Consulates Abroad

Algeria
05 Chemin Cheikh Bachir Ibrahimi, El-Biar 16030
Alger Algerie, Tel.: 213 (0) 770-08-2000

Argentina
Av. Colombia 4300, (C1425GMN) Buenos Aires
Tel.: (54-11) 5777-4533

Australia
Moonah Place, Yarralumla, ACT 2600, Tel. (02) 6214-5600

Bahrain
Bldg. 979, Road No. 3119, Block 321; Zinj District
Manama, Bahrain, Tel. (973)1724-2700; Consular (973)1724-2740

Belize
Floral Park Road, Belmopan, Cayo, Dial 011 +, Tel.: (501) 822-4011

Bolivia
Avenida Arce 2780, Casilla 425, La Paz, Tel.: (591) 2-216-8000

Brazil
SES – Av. das Nações, Quadra 801, Lote 03
70403-900 – Brasília, DF, Tel.: (55-61) 3312-7000

Canada
490 Sussex Drive, Ottawa, Ontario K1N 1G8, Tel: 613-688-5335

Chile
Av. Andrés Bello 2800, Las Condes, Santiago, Tel.: (56-2) 2330-3000

China
No. 55 An Jia Lou Lu 100600, Beijing, Tel: (86-10) 8531-3000

Colombia
Carrera 45 No. 24B-27 Bogotá, D.C., Tel.: (+57) (1) 275-2000

Costa Rica
Calle 98 Vía 104, Pavas, San José, Tel.: (506) 2519-2000

Democratic Republic of the Congo
310 Avenue des Aviateurs, Kinshasa, Gombe
Democratic Republic of the Congo, Tel.: 081 556-0151

Ecuador
E12-170 Avigiras Ave. and Eloy Alfaro Ave.Quito
Tel.: 593-2-398-5000

Egypt
(North Gate) 8, Kamal El-Din Salah St.
Garden City, Cairo, Tel.: (20-2) 797-3300

El Salvador
Final Boulevard Santa Elena, Antiguo Cuscatlán, La Libertad
Tel.: 2501-2999

Ethiopia
Entoto Street, P.O. Box 1014, Addis Ababa
Embassy Switchboard: 130-6000

Ghana
No. 24, Fourth Circular Rd., Cantonments, Accra
P.O. Box GP 2288, Accra, Ghana, Tel.: +233 (0) 30 274 1000

Guatemala
Avenida Reforma 7-01, Zona 10, Guatemala Ciudad
Tel.: (502) 2326-4000

Honduras
Avenida La Paz, Tegucigalpa M.D.C., Tel.: (504) 2236-9320

Iceland
Laufásvegur 21, 101 Reykjavík, Tel.: (354) 595 2200

India
Shantipath, Chanakyapuri, New Delhi 110021
Tel.: 011-91-11-2419-8000

Iran
U.S. Interests Section, Embassy of Switzerland
Africa Avenue, West Farzan St. No. 59
Tehran, Tel.: (98-21) 878-2964 and 879-2364

Iraq
APO AE 09316, Baghdad, Tel.: (00-1)240-553-0584 Ext. 5340 or 5635

Ireland, U.S. Consulate
Danesfort House, 223 Stranmillis Road, Belfast BT9 5GR
Tel.: [44] (0)28-9038-6100

Israel
14 David Flusser Street, Jerusalem 9378322, Tel.: 02-630-4000

Jordan
P.O. Box 354, Amman 11118, Tel.: (962-6) 590-6000

Kenya
United Nations Avenue Nairobi, P. O. Box 606 Village Market,
00621 Nairobi, Tel.: 254 20 363-6000

Kuwait
P. O. Box 77, Safat 13001, Tel.: (00-(965) 259-1001

Lebanon
Awkar-Facing the Municipality, Main Street, Beirut
Tel.: 04 – 543 600, Fax: 04 – 544 136

Mali
ACI 2000, Rue 243, Porte 297, Bamako, Tel.: +223 20 70 23 00

Morocco
Km 5.7, Avenue Mohamed VI, Souissi, Rabat 10170
Tel.: (212) 0537 637 200

Namibia
14 Lossen Street, Windhoek, Namibia, Tel.: 061-295-8500

New Zealand
29 Fitzherbert Terrace, Thorndon, Wellington 6011
Tel.: +64 4 462 6000

Nicaragua
Kilometer 5.5 Carretera Sur, Managua, Tel.: (505) 2252-7100

Nigeria
Plot 1075 Diplomatic Drive, Central District Area, Abuja
Tel.: (234)-9-461-4000

Oman
P.O.Box: 202, Pc: 115, Madinate Sultan Qaboos
Muscat, Tel.: (968) 24698-989

Panama
Building 783, Demetrio Basilio Lakas Avenue
Clayton, Panama City, Tel.: (507) 317-5000

Peru
Avenida La Encalada cdra. 17 s/n, Surco, Lima 33
Tel.: (51-1) 618-2000

Qatar
22nd February Street, Al-Luqta district, Doha, Tel.: (974)-488-4101

Russia
Bolshoy Deviatinsky, Pereulok No. 8
Moscow 121099, Russian Federation, Tel.: +7 (495) 728-5000

Rwanda
2657 Avenue de la Gendarmerie (Kacyiru),. P.O. Box 28 Kigali
Tel.: (250) 252 596 400

Saudi Arabia
P.O. Box 94309, Riyadh 11693, Tel.: 966-11-4883800

Scotland, U.S. Consulate
3 Regent Terrace, Edinburgh EH7 5BW, Tel.: [44] (0)131-556-8315

Senegal
Route des Almadies, Dakar, Tel.: (221) 33-879-4000

South Africa
877 Pretorius St, Arcadia, Pretoria
Tel.: +27 (12) 431-4000, Fax: +27 (12) 342-2299

South Sudan
Kololo Road, adjacent to the Europcan Union's compound, Juba

Sudan
P.O. Box 699, Kilo 10, Soba, Khartoum, Sudan
Tel.: (249)(187)-0-(22000), Within Sudan (187)-0-(22000)

Tanzania
686 Old Bagamoyo Road, Msasani, Dar es Salaam
Tel.: 255-22-229-4000

Tunisia
Les Berges du Lac, 1053 Tunis, Tel.: +216 71 107 000

Turkey
110 Atatürk Blvd., Kavaklıdere, 06100 Ankara, Tel.: (90-312) 455-5555

Uganda
1577 Ggaba Road, Kampala, Tel.: 256-414-259791

United Kingdom
33 Nine Elms Lane, London SW11 7US, Tel.: [44] (0)20 7499-9000

Venezuela
F St. and Suapure St., Urb. Colinas de Valle Arriba
Caracas, Venezuela 1080, Tel.: +58 (212) 975–6411

Yemen
Sa'awan Street, P.O. Box 22347. Sana'a, Yemen
Tel. (967) 1 755-2000 EXT. 2153 or 2266

Zimbabwe
172 Herbert Chitepo Ave, Harare, Zimbabwe, Tel: 263-4-250593/4

PARTING SHOT

Thank you so much for purchasing this book. You patronage fuels my adventures and keeps me writing. I appreciate all of you!

I always welcome feedback, comments, criticism, and testimonials as I continue to update all my books with the latest information I can find. This is often through the assistance of my readers, associates and friends including over 60 contributors on this book.

I also do keynote speaking on such topics as leadership, teamwork, and faith. Feel free to see if I am available for your next big event.

Say hi on Facebook www.facebook.com/treasurequestjack/ or send me an email at: jack@donorthmedia.com

Enjoy your travels and share your adventures so others and experience the beautiful world God created. Here is some travel wisdom from the Old Testament:

"The Lord keeps you from all harm and watches over your life. The Lord keeps watch over you as you come and go, both now and forever." Psalm 121:7-8

"If I rise on the wings of the dawn, if I settle on the far side of the sea, even there your hand will guide me, your right hand will hold me fast." Psalm 139:9-10

"Then you will go safely on your way, and you will not hurt your foot. When you lie down, you will not be afraid. As you lie there, your sleep will be sweet." Proverbs 3:23-24

Thank you,

Jack W. Peters

Made in the USA
Monee, IL
27 June 2022